I CALL YOU FRIENDS

THE PRIESTHOOD
MERCIFUL LOVE

CARDINAL JUSTIN RIGALI

LTP

LITURGY
TRAINING
PUBLICATIONS

I CALL YOU FRIENDS—THE PRIESTHOOD: MERCIFUL LOVE © 2004
Archdiocese of Chicago: Liturgy Training Publications, 1800 North
Hermitage Avenue, Chicago IL 60622-1101; 1-800-933-1800,
fax 1-800-933-7094, e-mail orders@ltp.org. All rights reserved.
Visit our website at www.ltp.org.

Printed in Canada.

Library of Congress Control Number 2004112515

ISBN 1-56854-554-1

FRIEND

To Mary
Mother of Mercy

Table of Contents

Addresses to Bishops

Dear brother Priests, dear Friends,

Jesus, the Good Shepherd, knew the hearts of His apostles. He knew their faith in Him, He knew their love for Him, and He trusted them. He called them His friends at the time when their sense of friendship was facing enormous challenges.

I Call You Friends presents many dimensions of our priesthood, our relationship with Jesus, with His people, with His Church. These are excerpts of homilies and talks given to my brother priests and some to my brother Bishops on various occasions and over a number of years. The occasions are generally not mentioned because all facets of our priesthood are woven into our daily lives. For our ongoing conversion we have to hear again and again the perennial truths of the Gospel.

I hope that in the midst of your daily challenges and burdens, the thoughts and reflections in this volume will recall and deepen the friendship to which Christ has personally called you.

When Jesus called us His friends, He also asked us to be united and to love one another as He loved each one of us. His presence is seen more readily in the midst of His people when His priests and His Bishops are more united (cf. *Lumen Gentium*, 21) in friendship, and in a greater understanding of each other's particular tasks in the common mission of His Church. Presenting talks given to both priests and Bishops in this one volume will hopefully help us all to support and appreciate one another more deeply, to strengthen our friendship and to rejoice together in the priesthood of Jesus Christ.

And so with joy and gratitude I call you *friends*.

+Justin Card. Rigali

1

Ordained To Be With Christ and To Be Sent Out

Dear brother Priests, dear Friends,

Recall the day when you awaited the laying on of hands and the outpouring of the Holy Spirit in the Sacrament of Holy Orders. You were gathered in the presence of family, friends, your brother seminarians, your brother priests, so many different representatives of the people of God. All assembled with you *in thanksgiving to God* for having sustained you throughout the years of your seminary preparation and for having brought you to that hour.

An Hour of Joy, Encouragement, and Hope

It was truly an *hour of joy* when the prayer of Jesus was fulfilled for you: "that my joy might be in you and your joy might be complete" (John 15:11).

It was *a time of encouragement for your brother priests:* to welcome you to the priesthood, to have your collaboration in their ministry and in the fraternity of the presbyterate.

It was *an hour of hope* for the Church. She was confident that the Christ who called you would call other generous men to His priesthood. We believe in the power of intercessory prayer; we believe in the power of Christ's

Paschal Mystery to draw young men to His priesthood in every age.

Called and Sent

You received your mission from our Lord Jesus Christ—
the One who has risen from the dead, the One who has triumphed over sin. In our midst, it is He—the Risen Christ—who, in and through the Church and in the power of the Holy Spirit, called you to the ministry of the priesthood. "As the Father has sent me"—Jesus said—"so I send you" (John 20:22).

Our Lord Jesus Christ was sending you out on that day on a mission that belongs to Him. It is *the mission of redemption*—redemption from sin, and consequently from death.

You were being called above all to become *ministers of the Eucharist.* The Second Vatican Council speaks to the world saying, "Priests fulfill their chief duty in the mystery of the Eucharistic Sacrifice. In it the work of our redemption continues to be carried out" (*Presbyterorum Ordinis,* 13). The work of the redemption is carried out because *in the Eucharist, the death and resurrection of the Lord Jesus Christ is renewed* for His people.

You belong to the priesthood that exists so that, in union with Christ and in the Holy Spirit, the people of God can adore the Father in spirit and in truth.

You exist for *conversion and holiness of life.* You exist, as does your priestly mission, so that God's people may live in holiness and walk in newness of life.

Invitation to Conversion and a Challenge of Love

In the very moment of Consecration, when the blood of the new and everlasting covenant is offered to the Father, the Church proclaims that this blood will be shed "so that sins may be forgiven."

In the very act of the Eucharist, you are *ministers of forgiveness*, as you offer up the Sacrifice of the Lamb, who takes away the sins of the world.

This ministry of forgiveness will be applied to individual hearts by *the Sacrament of Confession*, which is the Sacrament of Penance or the Sacrament of Reconciliation.

This *ministry of mercy* was extremely important to the Risen Christ on that first Easter, when He said. "Peace be with you. As the Father has sent me, so I send you. Receive the Holy Spirit. Whose sins you forgive are forgiven them, and whose sins you retain are retained" (John 20:22–23).

And so, both in the Eucharist and in Confession, *your ministry expresses the victory of Jesus over sin,* the victory whereby He purifies His people and frees them from the power of evil.

Hence, we are convinced, in the words of the Letter to the Hebrews, that "Every high priest is taken from among men and made their representative before God, to offer gifts and sacrifices for sins" (Hebrews 5:1). And we are further convinced that every priest "is able to deal patiently with the ignorant and erring, for he himself is beset by weakness and so, for this reason, must make sin offerings for himself as well as for the people."

Your gift to the Church requires both *an understanding of human weakness* and a willingness to launch an invitation to conversion and a challenge of love.

You yourselves need the Sacrament of Penance, and it is up to you to make it readily available to the people and to give them *the example of your own lives* of ongoing conversion. The humble recognition of your own weaknesses and sins must never be an excuse for ceasing to strive for holiness through a life of prayer.

The Eucharist—Source of All Pastoral Activity

In the Eucharist you will find the source of all your pastoral charity and the source of the joy that will be indispensable to your perseverance in the priesthood until death. Remember that the words of the Father spoken to Jesus will now apply to you: "You are a priest forever according to the order of Melchizedek" (Hebrews 5:6).

Your life as a priest must be consistent, and everything you do must be related to the Eucharist that you celebrate.

- Over and over again you proclaim the Gospel, but *your proclamation of the Gospel reaches its culmination in the Eucharistic sacrifice.*

- You give yourselves to *teaching the faith*, but those you teach can most effectively recognize and encounter Christ in the breaking of the bread.

- You devote yourselves to *the building of community*, but every community is united and fully one only when it shares the Eucharist.

- Your pastoral love must always be with the poor, the sick, with sinners, *with those in need of* love and hope and consolation, but Your effectiveness comes from your Eucharistic contact with the Risen Lord.

To Be With Jesus, To Be Sent Out

Remember how Jesus called His Apostles—Saint Mark tells us—first to be with Him, to experience His friendship, to know His love, to reflect on His teachings, and then to be sent out to proclaim the Gospel.

Dear brothers, this is your lot in life, your vocation: to be with Jesus and to be sent out to proclaim His Gospel. Alive in the power of the Holy Spirit, the Church had many things to ask of you on the day of your ordination, and she continues to do so every day of your life.

- She asks *fidelity* in your personal life, fidelity to prayer, to the Liturgy of the Hours—which is part of the praise and worship of the Church.

- She asks fidelity to the teachings of the Apostles as transmitted and interpreted by the living magisterium under the action of the Holy Spirit.

- She asks for you to *love and serve* in the name of Christ —to love all the people whom you are called to minister to in the name of Jesus, to love especially young brother priests, to stay close to them, to support them and be supported by them.

- The Church asks you to be just and courageous, merciful and chaste, and by your own lives to proclaim these virtues to others.

- The Church asks you to love Mary the Mother of Jesus and to learn constantly from her the mystery of her Son and the mystery of His Church.

And finally the Church asks you to trust—to trust in the power of the Paschal Mystery, to trust in the Risen Lord and in His strength. To trust that He who has begun a good work in you will bring it to fulfillment.

To trust that all the weaknesses and sins of the world are not equal to the power of the living Christ, who says to you today. "Peace be with you. . . . As the Father has sent me, so I send you. . . . Receive the Holy Spirit" (John 20:22–23).

Dear brothers, the people of God need you to exemplify and to proclaim total trust in the Christ who sends you, the Christ who loves you, the Christ who will sustain you forever.

2

Response to the Commandment of Love

Dear brother Priests, dear Friends,

At the very *center of the celebration* of the priesthood there is the proclamation of the words of Jesus: "It was not you who chose me, it was I who chose you and appointed you to go and bear fruit that will remain" (John 15:16).

And then these words are followed by that *solemn command of Jesus,* which spells out the meaning of everything that we are about: "This I command you: love one another" (John 15:17).

On the day of your ordination you presented yourselves with generosity and joy, in a *permanent commitment* that baffles and defies the world, to make this command of Christ the very substance of your lives forever! *"This I command you: love one another."*

And so the meaning of your ordination ceremony is all about *your response to the commandment of love*— a response that brings you into a ministry of service at the level of the priesthood. But this service begins with *a sacramental configuration to Jesus Christ,* Word made flesh and High Priest of our salvation.

The model of charity that is offered to you is *the love inherent in the Heart of Christ, Priest and Victim.* With this love you respond to His commandment of love. With this love you will *serve* and *serve* and *serve* until the end. This love is the love infused into the sacred humanity of Jesus by the anointing of the Holy Spirit.

The Spirit of the Lord Is Upon You

After the example of Jesus and in conformity to Him, you are called *to bring good tidings to the afflicted,* to heal the brokenhearted, to comfort all who mourn. The Lord Jesus proclaims through His word: "The Spirit of the Lord God is upon me, because He has anointed me" (Luke 4:18). And the Church authorizes you to proclaim this same mystery, this same great divine reality, which passes through your humanity.

In the Letter to the Hebrews, we are told how you are to exercise the love of Christ in the midst of the community: "Every high priest is taken from among men and made their representative before God, to offer gifts and sacrifices for sins (Hebrews 5:1).

This immediately brings us to the great sacrifice of the New Testament—*the Eucharist,* which, the Second Vatican Council assures all of us, is *the source and summit of our Christian lives,* and contains all the riches of the Church.

You Exist to Offer the Eucharist

And so you *exist to offer the Eucharist,* in and with the community of the Church, to offer the Eucharist for the living and the dead. You must never forget, as long as you live, those incisive words of the Second Vatican Council: "Priests fulfill their chief duty in the mystery of the Eucharistic Sacrifice. In it the work of our redemption continues to be carried out" (*Presbyterorum Ordinis,* 13).

The Letter to the Hebrews not only spells out *the role of the priest,* but it also tells us how to fulfill it. It says that the priest "is able to deal patiently with the ignorant and erring, for he himself is beset with weakness, and so, for this reason, must make sin offerings for himself as well as for other people" (Hebrews 5:2–3).

Bold, Fearless, and Merciful

In the community of the Church, and in unity of teaching with the Successor of Peter, the Bishop of Rome, and the Bishops in communion with him, *you must proclaim the Gospel* with all its *power,* in all its *purity,* with all its *exigencies.* With the conviction coming from God's Spirit, you must speak boldly and fearlessly, not out of human respect, divesting yourselves of any remnant of defensiveness in communicating the word of God. And yet, you shall *always deal gently with erring sinners,* with all your brothers and sisters, because you realize that you yourselves are beset by weakness and because you are bound to offer sacrifice for your own sins as well as for those of the people.

In this exhilarating context of the *consciousness of human weakness* you are called upon *to forgive sins in the name of Jesus.* One of His most precious gifts to the Church is the Sacrament of Penance, the Sacrament of Reconciliation, the Sacrament of Confession, the Sacrament of Mercy and Compassion—all inspired names to designate the great reality of salvation which is the fact that God, in His great mercy, forgives our sins, and, in His own plan, has willed to do so through Christ, through the ministry of His Church, and through the humanity of His priests.

The realization of human weakness leads you on to the *virtue of compunction,* to the *challenge of conversion,* to the *need for compassion* for the flock of Christ's Church.

In the Gospel we also hear these words of Jesus: "No one has greater love than this: to lay down one's life for one's friends" (John 15:13). Jesus the High Priest gives the example. For you, it is the meaning of the priesthood. There are many ways to exercise it—all related to the Eucharist.

Communicate the God Whom You Seek

Your holiness of life and the challenge constantly to seek God and to be converted to Him are supremely relevant to your priesthood. You will only be able to communicate the God whom you have sought and found in Jesus Christ and whom you possess in holiness of life.

In the very rite of Ordination to the Priesthood during the prayer of consecration, as the Church invoked upon you *the Spirit of God,* she did so calling Him the "Spirit of holiness." The Church prayed that the Spirit of holiness would renew you for the mission of the priesthood, for the proclamation of the Gospel at its highest level, which is the Eucharist, and for the salvation of the world.

In this context, dear friends, dear brothers, *your response to God, your prayer, your commitment to the Divine Office, your response to God's commandment of love* are so important. To help you, Mary the Mother of Jesus, the Mother of His Church, the Mother of His priests is with you always.

And remember always, in moments of strength and weakness, in moments of joy and pain, in moments of hope and human discouragement that *the Jesus who commands you to love one another is the Jesus who supports you,* the Jesus who sustains you, the Jesus who loves you and all those to whom you minister.

It is He, our Lord Jesus Christ, who repeats deeply in your hearts: "It was not you who chose me, but I who chose you and appointed you to go and bear fruit that will remain" (John 15:16).

3

Being Together

Dear brother Priests, dear Friends,

Our being together is an extremely important dimension of our priesthood—the priesthood that we share with Christ. Besides the fact that Christ said, "Where two or three are gathered together in my name" (Matthew 18:20), we also have that *powerful example* in the call of the Apostles as related by Saint Mark in his third chapter. He explains how Jesus went up the mountain and how He chose the Apostles, first of all *to be with Him,* and secondly, *to be sent out.* To be with Him and to be sent out! Well, I am convinced that to be with Him meant also *to be with each other* in the solidarity of discipleship, in the unity of the priesthood, in the joy of companionship, fraternity, and community, and in the hope of being supported, loved, and sustained for the mission of proclaiming the Gospel of salvation in the name of Christ—the One who calls us and invites us by the power of His Spirit for the glory of His Father.

Being Together with Christ and in Christ

This is, and must increasingly become, our *common vision*—being together, being with Christ. This explains its importance; why we put so much effort into it, and why we place so much hope in its results. I cannot emphasize enough *the value of being together*—of being together with Christ and in Christ. At times we must leave behind us very important duties, commitments, engagements, pressing pastoral business. And we do this for a purpose and with justification. These are not just days off. These are times of sharing among ourselves our life, our priesthood, and everything that makes it up.

Being together in Christ, we are strengthening and consolidating a *common vision of our priesthood*. Not starting, though, from scratch but continually listening to the Holy Spirit as He speaks in the word of God, as He speaks in our various and differing experiences as a local Church, and in the experiences of the one universal Church. As He speaks through the Councils, especially Vatican II, through the College of Bishops, and the teaching of its head, the Bishop of Rome. As He speaks through so many authentically profound intuitions of our people who say to us what the Greeks said to Philip, as we see in the Gospel of Saint John: "We would like to see Jesus" (John 12:20).

We are called to *listen to each other, to share one another's experiences*—our experiences in the priesthood. Sharing the hopes and joys, the successes, the sufferings, anxieties, sometimes the frustrations and depression of our brother priests. It means *mutual support* in shared weaknesses and inevitable failings. Not inevitable *failure*, but inevitable failings. Mutual support is inspired by and inspires *hope in the strength and power of Christ's Paschal Mystery*.

We give and receive mutual support, that fraternal support of brothers who have themselves received the divine support of mercy, compassion and forgiveness, as well as *the call to hope, the call to prayer, the call to conversion*.

We open our hearts to answer the call in order to be in a position ever more effectively *to help shepherd the flock*.

As we do this, we will be conscious of the diversity of God's gifts in all of us—the gifts yet to be fully developed, yet to be fully utilized for one single mission of service. And the more we realize our diversity of gifts in the unity of the priesthood, the more we will give thanks to God and be confirmed in mutual esteem and fraternal love, the more we will be happy to be together in the unity of our priesthood— to be together with Christ and to be sent out—to be sent out on a mission, a very arduous and consuming mission.

With these sentiments our coming together makes a great deal of sense, and it is more than justified. And just as we leave aside so many worthy pastoral activities to be together, we suspend also, for a few moments, concentration on some of our personal and pastoral concerns in order to concentrate our attention on what is so much a part of our life and ministry as priests: *"Evangelization"* and everything that this implies.

Challenges of Evangelization

I wish to assure you that *I share with you* all the many concerns of the presbyterate. It is my hope *to pray with you,* to try to address together as effectively as we can, with God's help, the specific concerns and challenges that are connected with our priestly life and ministry.

As we face the future together, it is important to realize that God has infused into the presbyterate *a collection of marvelous gifts and graces.* We have a history of God's sustaining help in all the circumstances and situations that have affected our people's lives for generations. We have experienced the care of our Blessed Mother Mary over the years—so many of our parishes have been dedicated to her under her different titles—and we are proud of what

God has accomplished in our midst. Everywhere we see *the action of the Holy Spirit calling people to conversion of heart* so that they may communicate Christ, and love and serve the world with His charity and zeal. Everywhere we go, however, we meet different types of obstacles to evangelization. But even here we are conscious that we are part of an apostolic tradition. Saint Paul spells out for us a long list of his own difficulties — those things that made his own ministry so arduous, those things that were constantly a challenge to his zeal and a challenge to his faith and trust. I am thinking of 2 Corinthians 11:23 ff. — the long list of difficulties that he had to encounter and that never went away.

In another context, in his Letter to the Romans he poses the question, "What will separate us from the love of Christ?" Will anguish, or distress, or persecution, or famine, or nakedness, or peril, or the sword?" and he answers, ". . . in all these things we are conquerors overwhelmingly through him who loved us" (Romans 8:35–37).

At the Level of Faith

As priests all of us also have *our clear personal limitations,* our human weaknesses, our infirmities, our inconsistencies, and our sins. But balancing all of this is *the strength of Christ.* Our human condition is meant to be. And just as we cannot separate ourselves from it, neither can we separate ourselves totally from the obstacles and difficulties inherent in this condition and accompanying it. But where does this leave us? At the level of faith. Once again Saint Paul puts it very well: ". . . a thorn in the flesh was given to me, an angel of Satan, to beat me, to keep me from being too elated. Three times I begged the Lord about this, that it might leave me, but he said to me, 'My grace is sufficient for you, for power is made perfect in weakness.' I will rather boast most gladly of my weaknesses, in order that the power of Christ might dwell in me." "Therefore," Saint Paul continues, "I am content with weaknesses, insults, hardships, persecutions, and constraints, for the sake of Christ; for when I am weak, then I am strong" (2 Corinthians 12:7–10).

My dear brother priests, I believe that Saint Paul is offering us a very important part of our view of the priesthood—what the priesthood is all about: the power of Christ—the power of Christ to uplift, to sustain, to forgive, to heal. And we priests admit, or—to use the term of Saint Paul—"boast" of our weaknesses and difficulties— not to remain in them, but to rise above them by the power of Christ.

What is true of our personal weaknesses is true, also, of *the limitations of our structures.* We must resolutely endeavor to perfect them, but all the while realizing that all our efforts depend upon the strength of Christ for their supernatural effectiveness. In all of this, we must continue to work together.

A very great and wonderful, although imperfect reality that is so much a part of our lives is the *parish*, with its many hopes and challenges, its many joys and difficulties. It is in the parish that the main work of evangelization takes place. It is in and from the parish that so many of our concerns arise. Even in the future we are convinced that any concerns will never surpass the hopes and joys of our parish families.

4

In Our Identity and Mission We Are Not Alone!

Dear brother Priests, dear Friends,

I am always grateful to my brother priests for responding to the Church's invitation to come together, under the sign of the holiness of Christ's priesthood, to a *Day of Prayer for the Sanctification of Priests*. This invitation comes to us through our Holy Father Pope John Paul II and puts us in communion with our brother priests throughout the world.

The fact that we can gather together as both diocesan and religious priests reminds us that we have a single priesthood, a single mission. I am always grateful to all of you for the efforts that you make, for giving this gathering a *priority* in your busy lives.

We are grateful for the grace to be together in prayer, to have the opportunity for reconciliation in the Sacrament of Penance, and to reflect on God's word and on the priesthood of Christ.

Our Identity, Our Mission, Our Holiness

The word of God forcefully speaks to us about *our identity and our mission*. Like Saint Paul we are compelled to preach the Gospel. With him each of us can say,

"Woe to me if I do not preach it!" (1 Corinthians 9:16) Like him, we find our identity in being "the slave of all" (1 Corinthians 9:19) giving everything we have and everything we are in order to proclaim the Good News of Jesus Christ.

From the Gospel words of Jesus, we know, however, that we cannot lead blindly. We cannot speak hypocritically to others about holiness, about justice, about the truth of their relationship with God and with others unless we ourselves are trying earnestly and perseveringly to be holy. We recognize *our own call to holiness,* our need for union with Jesus, for bonding with Christ the Priest. We are not pretending that we have reached our goal or that we can ever reach it on our own, but we are acknowledging that Christ is calling us to holiness and is able to bring it about in our lives. We remember the expression of Saint Paul, how Jesus became sin for us, so that we might become the very holiness of God.

We already know this in our hearts, but Vatican II wanted to remind us that "priestly holiness itself contributes very greatly to a fruitful fulfillment of the priestly ministry" (*Presbyterorum Ordinis,* 12). Vatican II also wanted to help us understand our own spirituality, how we attain it, what it means. And so the Council says: "Thus by assuming the role of the Good Shepherd, priests will find in the very exercise of pastoral love the bond of priestly perfection which will unify their lives and activities. This pastoral love flows mainly from the Eucharistic Sacrifice, which is therefore the center and root of the whole priestly life" (*ibid.,* 14).

What a great consolation to know that *holiness for us is bound up with our ministry and flows from the Eucharist.* To share fully in the Eucharist obviously requires lives of prayer and discipline, which in turn sustain and give joy to our daily priestly activities.

We Are Never Alone

To be what we are supposed to be is a big challenge. It requires so much strength. We know this and so does Jesus. We must come together, to pray with Him. It is very important not to be alone. *We need Christ. We need each other.*

In the Gospels Christ tells us that *He is not alone.* He experiences communion with His Father: "The one who sent me is with me; He has not left me alone . . ." (John 8:29). On another occasion Jesus says, "I am not alone, because the Father is with me" (John 16:32). Christ's consciousness of being one with His Father pervades His life and mission. It is a source of strength for Him. Even at the height of His Passion, He knows that He is not abandoned, even though He suffers in His human nature the anguish of loneliness. Christ also knows that all His disciples, including us priests, have the same need that He had. *We are not expected to face our mission alone.* And so Christ promised, "I am with you always, until the end of the age" (Matthew 28:20). These words are an echo of promises that God made before.

In the history of salvation God never abandoned those to whom He entrusted a mission. Moses heard God say, "I will be with you" (Exodus 3:12). Jeremiah, who was so fearful of the prophetic task, was reassured by God, "I am with you to deliver you" (Jeremiah 1:18). Saint Paul also heard reassuring words: "Do not be afraid, go on speaking and do not be silent, for I am with you . . ." (Acts 18:9).

We joyfully celebrate the wonderful conviction of Christ about Himself: "I am not alone." This is our conviction too as we strive to rise to the challenge of holiness in order to be able to proclaim the Gospel, worthily, sincerely, effectively. *Like Christ, we are not alone.* We have His support, the communion of His Father, the power of His Spirit.

We are not alone. *We have each other* in the oneness of the priesthood, in the unity of the presbyterate.

We are not alone. *We have the love and support of God's people,* the prayers of our communities.

We are not alone. We belong to a worldwide Church in a solidarity which is both a consolation and a challenge to how we live and think and act.

We are not alone today, nor shall we ever be alone. In our joys and sufferings, in our pastoral activities and challenges, in our moments of weakness and strength, *the Lord Jesus is close to us,* confirming us in our call to holiness, in our service to life, in our ministry of proclaiming the Gospel.

Thanks be to God: We are not alone.

5

Who Are the Workers?

Dear brother Priests, dear Friends,

As priests we are deeply concerned with the question: "Who are the workers of evangelization?" One of the greatest results of the Second Vatican Council is the ever more widespread realization that the work of evangelization is a basic duty of the people of God. Our evangelizing role, our evangelizing powers as priests are special and correspond to the will of Christ. But evangelization belongs to the whole Church. How important is our service of involving the religious and laity in the single mission of evangelization and, consequently, of human advancement! What magnificent opportunities are open to us as we work together with families, young people, the sick, and every category of the faithful to proclaim Christ's love! We shall always endeavor to collaborate as much as possible with all our other Christian brothers and sisters. All of us realize that the evangelizer is not the absolute master of evangelizing action. This belongs, rather, to the Church and we have the great responsibility and privilege of preserving and transmitting unaltered the content of the Church's Catholic faith in a way adapted to the needs of the times.

As we reflect on our special priestly call to evangelize, we willingly admit the absolute need for the action of the Holy Spirit. The task is so much bigger than we are.

The Church reminds us forcefully—"Techniques of evangelization are good, but even the most advanced ones could not replace the gentle action of the Spirit. The most perfect preparations of the evangelizer have no effect without the Holy Spirit. Without the Holy Spirit, the most convincing dialectic has no power over the human heart. Without the Holy Spirit, the most highly developed schemas resting on a sociological or psychological basis are quickly seen to be quite valueless" (*Evangelii Nuntiandi*, 75).

The Holy Spirit teaches us to be patient with ourselves and to trust in Him. At the same time He teaches us that certain structures in our Church will never be more perfect than we ourselves. Hence, once again, for each of us an important aspect of evangelization is the call to conversion, the call to prayer, the call to holiness of life.

To Evangelize by Promoting Vocations

In proposing for our reflection and for the inspiration of our priesthood, the call to evangelize, I would like to invite all priests to a renewed effort in prayer and action to discover and foster new vocations to the priesthood.

All evangelizing activity is linked to this mystery of Christ's love. In a very real way, the challenge to evangelize becomes the challenge of promoting vocations. I ask for your renewed help and commitment to vocations.

In the first place, we must show our firm trust in the power of Jesus Christ's Paschal Mystery to raise up young men willing to dare to follow the Lord in celibate love. Working together we will succeed through prayer and the joyful witness of loving the priesthood—as well as through all the other creative means available to us. The spirit of our call must endure: We love the priesthood; we are happy to be priests—to be with Christ and to be sent out—and we want young men to experience this joy, which is always greater than all the difficulties inherent in our life and ministry. Jesus explicitly invited men to follow Him. In His name we must do the same. And we must do this with joy, love, and zeal, commending our efforts to Mary the Mother of Christ our Priest.

We Are Loved and Therefore We Love!

There are many other things that I would like to share with you in faith and love: our need to support one another in our spiritual lives, the importance of emphasizing God's mercy and proclaiming it in the Sacrament of Penance, and also, the importance of the *Catechism of the Catholic Church* in our evangelizing ministry. In these activities and in everything else that we do together for the Gospel, let us renew our trust in Christ who called us. On my part, I am deeply grateful for your partnership in the Gospel, for your lives of faith and labor of love.

Through the power of the Spirit, the Lord Jesus is in our midst to sustain us today and always. Let us go forward together, dear brothers in the priesthood—forward together to meet the call to evangelization, the call to prayer, the call to conversion and holiness of life.

And, let us not be afraid, because we are loved and, therefore, we love!

6

Gift and Mystery

Dear brother Priests, dear Friends,

It is indeed a joy to recall and celebrate our ordination to the priesthood. For the Church, ordination is a time of hope and renewal. For us, to recall it in prayer is a moment of renewed consecration to Jesus Christ, our great High Priest, and of commitment to the mission of the seventy-two disciples that we see portrayed in the Gospel. Like the seventy-two and as one of their successors in the community, we are ordained to proclaim—in word and sacrament, especially in the Eucharist, in deed and by example—the Kingdom of God. We have been chosen by Christ for a special mission at the service of His community, to be exercised in His name and in His sacred person.

To Be a Priest

Let us reflect for a few moments on what it means for each of us to be a priest.

Some time ago a new book hit the market—three quarters of a million copies in the first printing. It was entitled *Gift and Mystery*. It is the personal story of the vocation to the priesthood of Pope John Paul II.

The Pope explains how the priesthood is truly a gift of God; it is also a mystery—a divine reality—something that we can never thoroughly fathom. This gift takes its

origin from Christ's love; it is given for the good of the
whole community, but it is entrusted to individual men.

After fifty years of priestly life, the Pope explains what
this gift has meant for him. He takes us back to the early
years of his priesthood: the work in his first parish, his
sacramental ministry, all his pastoral activities, his work on
behalf of justice and human dignity, his service to and with
the laity, his special love for families struggling to fulfill
their vocation and to be holy. He speaks about the place
of prayer in his life, the assistance and support he received
from brother priests, and the love and strength that he
always found in the Immaculate Heart of Mary.

To Be Able to Celebrate Mass Everyday

At the center of his ministry there has always been
the Eucharist. He explains repeatedly what it means to him
and to every priest.

On one occasion a journalist approached the Pope
with observations and questions. He mentioned that, as
Pope, John Paul II certainly has to deal with problems. But
he also added that the Pope must indeed have many joys.
And then he asked what the greatest of them was. The Holy
Father responded right away and explained that his greatest
joy was to have the privilege that belongs to every priest
in the world—to be able to celebrate Mass every day.

And this is what we are ordained to do. We have
read the documents of Vatican II. We remember what
it says about the priest and his relationship to the Eucharist.
We recall that the Council says that all our "pastoral love
flows mainly from the Eucharistic Sacrifice, which is therefore the center and root of the whole priestly life."

And then we remember another quote of Vatican II that says, "priests fulfill their chief duty in the mystery of the Eucharistic Sacrifice. In it the work of our redemption continues to be carried out. For this reason," the Council goes on to say, "the priests are strongly urged to celebrate Mass every day, for even if the faithful are unable to be present, it is an act of Christ and the Church." And how beautiful it is when we are gathered with a community, day after day, to carry on the work of redemption and build up the Kingdom of God.

The Love of Christ Impels Us

For this reason the Spirit of the Lord God is upon us and the Lord anoints us to bring the Gospel to the poor and to heal the brokenhearted, to minister to so many who need our help.

And the ideal of our priesthood is also expressed in the reading from Saint Paul: "The love of Christ impels us" (2 Corinthians 5:14)—the love of the One who died for all, so that all may live and die in Christ.

At the end of his book, the Pope goes on to explain how important it is—drawing strength from the Eucharist—to work with the laity and to serve the families of the Church. And finally he explains how every priest is sent out to discover other vocations to the priesthood, just as we have been discovered by Christ and the Church.

The Church is grateful for the gift of the priesthood that we have received, and she is grateful to all those who have sustained us and helped us by their love, their friendship, and their support. Above all, the Church thanks God for having brought us to the holy day of ordination to the priesthood of Jesus Christ.

7

Fulfillment and Joy

Dear brother Priests, dear Friends,

The Second Vatican Council tells us that when the word of God is proclaimed in the liturgy *Jesus Christ Himself is present* in the action of His Church and speaks to His people.

Jesus Christ speaks to all of us in every word that we hear proclaimed in the Gospels. In a very real way He says to His chosen ones and to each of us: "All this I tell you that my joy might be in you and your joy might be complete" (John 15:11). Everything about our priesthood is touched *by the joy that comes from the Heart of Jesus!* We are filled with joy because the prophecy spoken of Jesus is also being fulfilled in us: "The Spirit of the Lord is upon me, because the Lord has anointed me; He has sent me to bring glad tidings to the lowly, to heal the brokenhearted" (Isaiah 61:1). This joy is contagious! It permeates the hearts of all, especially those who have shared in the lives of priests, those who have encouraged us and prayed for us. It is our prayer that the joy of the day of our ordination will never be eclipsed and that as priests we will live up to the challenge of Vatican II, which urges all priests to be "radiant with the spirit of service and true paschal joy" (*Presbyterorum Ordinis*, 11).

For You, Personally

It is true that every word of Scripture is meant for all of us. But it is also true that the words of Scripture are directed in a deeply personal way to priests. For this reason I ask you to reflect with me on the word of God, and to receive it very personally.

Dear brother priests, Jesus is speaking to you *a message that you must not miss:* "As the Father loves me, so I also love you. Remain in my love. If you keep my commandments, you will live in my love" (John 15:9–10). Jesus then tells you what His special commandment is: "This is my commandment: love one another as I love you" (John 10:17–18).

The type of love that Jesus is speaking of to you is *pastoral love*. He explains: "No one has greater love than this: to lay down one's life for one's friends" (John 15:13). This is the conclusion to which the Gospel is leading you: to lay down your life, the way Christ laid down His life, *as priest and victim.*

Reflect for a few moments on another passage from Saint John's Gospel, chapter 10, where Jesus talks about *laying down His life.* In that passage Jesus emphasized two things: 1) He is loved by His Father because He lays down His life, and 2) He lays it down freely—He has the power to do that. His words are, "This is why the Father loves me, because I lay down my life. . . . I lay it down on my own. I have power to lay it down" (John 10:17–18).

Dear brothers, Jesus' words apply to you. *The Father loves you because you lay down your life.* You do it *freely.* You do it on your own. You have *the power* to do it.

• *What tremendous love you are receiving* from the Father!

- *What great power you are exercising* in giving your life freely in celibacy for your friends—all those whom you love in Jesus Christ.

Dear brothers, with the passing of years in the priesthood, some of the exhilaration characteristic of the moment of your ordination passes. But *the Father's love* will never be diminished, nor will *your power* decrease to be able to lay down your life—freely—for your friends. And *the commandment to love one another will always be the same.* For you this means *a life of pastoral charity expressed in service to God's people.*

Eucharistic Pastoral Charity

In this regard the Second Vatican Council has some very important advice for you and me and all our brother priests. It says that we must find *the main source of all our pastoral charity in the Eucharistic Sacrifice* of the Mass, which is the center and root of our priestly lives (cf. *loc. cit.,* 14). Our days are filled with many other activities besides the Eucharist, but when the Eucharist is lacking, so too is the main source of our pastoral charity. The Church is counting on our pastoral charity as we go forth to proclaim the Gospel, to forgive sins, and to heal the brokenhearted in the name of Jesus.

We are being sent by Christ to the poor, to those in need, to those who are asking for compassion, for justice, for human dignity, for truth—the truth about God, about Christ, about eternal life. Try to remember the words of Pope John Paul II who tells us, "The priest's special love will always be with the sick and dying, with those in pain and sorrow, and those in sin. For every Bishop and priest there is but one ideal—the person who says, 'I am the good

shepherd . . . and I lay down my life for the sheep'"
(Address to the Bishops of the United States, September 9,
1983). Dear brothers, this is our life of pastoral charity.
With it comes fulfillment and joy.

In concluding its treatment of priestly life and
ministry, Vatican II realistically speaks about *the difficulties*
inherent in such a vocation. Scripture confirms this by
speaking to us of our human condition and its many limitations. A consciousness of our condition calls us to both
compassion and humility. This is the way the author of
the Letter to the Hebrews sees the priests. In his work, the
priest "is able to deal patiently with the ignorant and erring,
for he is himself beset by weakness and so, for this reason,
must make sin offerings for himself as well as for other
people" (Hebrews 5:1). Since the Eucharist is our sin offering,
we see once again how it penetrates every dimension of our
priesthood, supporting our weaknesses and giving us hope.

In drawing attention to the difficulties and challenges of the priesthood, Vatican II urges us to realize that
we are *not alone.* Jesus Christ is with us, encouraging us
and telling us, "Take courage, I have conquered the world"
(John 16:33). And He has given us the support of *our*
people, with their innate respect and esteem and love for
the priesthood as it comes forth from the Heart of Christ.
And then Christ has given us *each other:* It is the gift of
belonging to the presbyterate, expressing our unity and communion in the faith and love of the Church!

Finally there is *Mary, the Mother of Jesus* our great
High Priest. She gave humanity to the Son of God, who
became a priest in her womb. She showed Him a Mother's
love until the end of His life. She does the same for each
one of us. By her prayers she assists us to persevere in joy and
to grasp more fully every day what Jesus meant when He

said, "No one has greater love than this, to lay down one's life for one's friends" (John 15:13). There is no greater love and no greater joy!

8

Do You Love Me?
Feed My Lambs . . .
Tend My Sheep

Dear brother Priests, dear Friends,

For a few moments let us reflect as priests on some
of the many aspects of the mystery we are living in faith.
Permit me to begin with a personal reflection. It was some
years ago that Mother Teresa of Calcutta received an
international Peace Prize. On that occasion there was a
reception held for her in the Vatican at which I was present.
She was to speak to dozens of Ambassadors from around
the world. Before the event, in which I was involved, I
asked Mother Teresa what she was going to talk about. She
responded to me very simply, saying that she did not know
but that she was going to speak about *Jesus*. And so she
did—eloquently, simply, convincingly. For Mother Teresa,
the Jesus to whom she bore witness is the person of
the Eternal Word, the Son of God, the Son of Mary, the
Jesus present in the Blessed Sacrament, but also the Jesus
present in the poor and suffering, and in those in every
sort of need.

Pastoral Charity: Feeding Christ's Lambs

Our specific vocation is to proclaim Jesus Christ, to respond to His love, so often manifested in our lives, and to accept ever more His invitation to love Him.

"Do you love me?" These words certainly resound in our own hearts. And so must the challenge of Jesus: "Feed my lambs . . . Feed my sheep" (John 21:15–16).

We have embraced a sacred ministry by which we are enabled to do just this: to collaborate in feeding Christ's lambs, in feeding His sheep, in serving the people of God.

Our vocation to the priesthood of Jesus Christ confirms us in our Christian vocation of discipleship.

Our commitment with all our brothers and sisters in the Church to mutual love and generous service is ratified and reinforced, as Saint Paul says, "Above all, let your love for one another be intense. . . . as each one has received a gift, use it to serve one another as good stewards of God's varied grace" (1 Peter 4:8–10).

Because we are called to the *ministerial priesthood*, we are called to the vocation of *pastoral love*. Our response to Christ's call, "Feed my lambs, tend my sheep," has a specific configuration. We are called to love and serve in a new way, to contribute to building up the Kingdom of God as priests, to proclaim Jesus Christ in different ways but above all in a sacramental and salvific way. Hence the Second Vatican Council tells us, "Priests fulfill their chief duty in the mystery of the Eucharistic Sacrifice. In it the work of our redemption continues to be carried out" (*Presbyterorum Ordinis*, 13). At the same time Vatican II assures us that the source of our pastoral charity—which we exercise in countless ways—is found in the Eucharist. For this reason Vatican II states that "priests are strongly urged to celebrate

Mass every day," adding that "even if the faithful are unable to be present, it is an act of Christ and the Church."

Proclaiming the Message of the One Who Sent Us

The Church, who mediates and confirms our vocation, charges us to proclaim the word of God in season and out of season. We are sent in order to communicate the unspeakable riches of Christ to the community, and particularly to the poor, who are special for us as they were for Christ.

With Christ we are servants and evangelizers. Our greatest service is evangelization, which finds its source and summit in the Eucharist. With Christ and in His Church we are ministers of reconciliation, proclaiming mercy and pardon and forgiveness for sins. We are builders of community—on the one foundation Jesus Christ. We are teachers in the Church, to speak with the love of Christ and in accordance with the wisdom of His Church. As we proclaim the Paschal Mystery of Christ's death and resurrection, and His whole Gospel of life, sometimes we have to part ways with the majority opinion, with unanimous verdicts, and with politically correct positions. We are always called upon to remember that Jesus says: "My teaching is not my own but is from the one who sent me" (John 7:16).

In speaking about the pastoral charity of priests, Pope John Paul II says, "The priest's special love will always be with the sick and dying, with those in pain and sorrow, and with those in sin." And he adds, "For every Bishop and every priest there is but one ideal—the person who says, 'I am the good shepherd . . . and I lay down my life for the sheep'" (*Ad Limina* Address of September 9, 1983).

Vast new horizons and possibilities open up for us as we speak about Jesus, as we proclaim His death and resurrection and the pardon and merciful love that flows from them.

The community of the Church is with us in prayer and pledges us support and love as we respond faithfully, generously, perseveringly to the question of Jesus: "Do you love me?" and we strive to meet His challenge and fulfill His words: "Feed my lambs . . . tend my sheep."

9

To Evangelize and
To Be Evangelized

Dear brother Priests, dear Friends,

The Church is born of the evangelizing activity of Jesus and the Twelve. It becomes an evangelizer, but begins by being evangelized.

Pope Paul VI with the Synod of Bishops asked, and wanted us to ask ourselves, *"What is evangelization and what does it involve?"* The simplicity of the answer is powerful. "For the Church evangelization means bringing the Good News into all the strata of humanity and through its influence transforming humanity from within and making it new" (*Evangelii Nuntiandi*, 18). Evangelization consists, then, in proclaiming Christ to those who do not know Him; in preaching His message with all its demands in catechesis—the teaching and maturation stage—and in the gift of the sacraments.

In speaking about evangelizing all the strata of humanity, the Exhortation *Evangelii Nuntiandi* goes on to say: "For the Church it is a question not only of preaching the Gospel in ever wider geographic areas or to ever greater numbers of people, but also of affecting and, as it were, upsetting through the power of the Gospel, humanity's criteria of judgment, determining values, points of interest, lines of thought, sources of inspiration, and models of life which are in contrast with the word of God and the plan of salvation" (*ibid.*, 19). For this reason we see how relevant to evangelization is our *ministry of charity* and *social justice,* our efforts to educate, for *international solidarity,* and all our *pro-life activities.*

At every turn, however, the Gospel must be proclaimed *by witness.* And the witness of true and persevering love, of true and persevering commitment to action must be sustained by prayer. Back in 1976 there was a meeting in Detroit—the Call to Action Congress. And at that time Pope Paul VI encouraged the Call to Action to be the launching of a whole new social consciousness of service. But he made the important point that in the long tradition of the Church *any call to action is first of all a call to prayer.*

Another particular type of *witness* that upsets the criteria of the world, especially at this time, and for which prayer is so indispensable, is *celibacy* that is embraced for the Kingdom of God and the salvation of the world. Many times since the Second Vatican Council the Church has appealed to us priests precisely to encourage us in our perseverance to recognize, despite our human weakness, how great a witness we bear by celibacy to the primacy of God.

The finest witness in the Church is, however, insufficient and in the long run will prove ineffective if it is not explained "and made explicit by *a clear and unequivocal proclamation of the Lord Jesus.*" The Good News proclaimed by the witness of life sooner or later has to be proclaimed by the word of life. "There is no true evangelization," and these words of Pope Paul VI are extremely important, "if the name, the teaching, the life, the promises, the Kingdom and the mystery of Jesus of Nazareth, the Son of God, are not proclaimed" (*ibid.*, 22).

Offering God's Mercy in Jesus

The *content* of evangelization hence takes on for us in our ministry a great significance. In *Evangelii Nuntiandi* we are reminded that evangelization "will always contain— as the foundation, center and at the same time, summit of its dynamism—a clear proclamation that in Christ, the Son of God made man who died and rose from the dead, *salvation is offered to all as a gift of God's grace and mercy in Jesus*" (*ibid.*, 27). The Church urges us to proclaim not an immanent salvation, but one that embraces, yet exceeds, temporal desires, hopes, affairs, and struggles—a transcendent and eschatological salvation which indeed has its beginning in this life, but which is fulfilled in the communion of the Blessed Trinity.

Saint Matthew summarizes the evangelizing activity of Jesus in these words: "He went around all of Galilee, teaching in their synagogues, *proclaiming the gospel of the Kingdom* and *curing the people* of every disease and illness" (Matthew 4:23). What an inspiration these words have been in the history of the Church and must continue to be! They explain and motivate all our teaching, our proclamation and *our total involvement* in all the human needs of our people.

Our evangelization takes on an extremely important dimension of hope. As the Church waits in joyful hope, in the expression of our liturgy, for the coming of our Savior Jesus Christ, she proclaims the new commandment of love. "This is my commandment: love one another as I love you" (John 15:12).

Because of the marvel of the Incarnation—the Word became Flesh—"evangelization would not be complete," Pope Paul VI tells us, "if it did not take account of the *unceasing interplay of the Gospel and the concrete life of the human being,* both personal and social. That is why evangelization involves an explicit message adapted to the different situations constantly being realized, about *the rights and duties of every human being,* about *family life* without which personal growth and development is hardly possible, about *life in society,* about *international life, peace, justice and development,* a message especially energetic today, about *liberation*" (*ibid.,* 29).

At the basis of all of this is the fact that God so loved the world that He sent His Son, and *the Son sent us to proclaim this love*—this incarnate love—and to bear witness to it in the power of the Holy Spirit. While reaffirming the primacy of her spiritual vocation, the Church can never disassociate herself from temporal problems. Hence, she recognizes that *between evangelization and human advancement*—which includes both *development and liberation*—there are in fact profound links. The plan of creation cannot be separated from the plan of redemption. The *defense of human dignity* and all human rights, especially the right to life, must always form part of our evangelizing activity.

For the Church it is important for structures to be built up "which are more human, more just, more respectful of the rights of the human person and less oppressive and less enslaving, but she is conscious that the most idealized systems soon become inhuman if the inhuman inclinations of the human heart are not made wholesome, if those who live in these structures, or who rule them, do not undergo a conversion of heart and outlook" (*ibid.,* 36). All of this applies to us.

Called to Conversion of Heart and Holiness of Life

Hence, *we return always to the need for personal conversion,* to the need to preach conversion, to be converted ourselves. This is the exact point where the Gospel begins. Jesus calls us to conversion of heart and holiness of life.

When we speak of the methods of evangelization, we will always have to start out with the *witness* of an authentic Christian life, the witness of an authentic priestly life. It is encouraging for us to find so many of our activities among the Church's principal methods of evangelization: preaching, the liturgy of the word, catechetics, the use of the mass media, personal contacts.

The Church wants us to understand who are the *beneficiaries* of our evangelization. And Jesus Himself makes it clear that we are to proclaim the Good News to all creation. *Our spirit must be missionary.* What is at stake is the nature of the Gospel and the nature of the Church.

The Church also goes on record as pointing out, above all today, that neither respect nor esteem for non-Christian religions, which must of course always be present, is an invitation to Christians to withhold from non-Christians the proclamation of Jesus Christ as the Son of God, the one Mediator and the Savior of the whole world (cf. *ibid.,* 53).

10

Free to Lay Down Our Lives

Dear brother Priests, dear Friends,

We remember how Christ chose the first apostles "to be with Him" and "to be sent out." We have been sent out and have all experienced the burdens of the apostolic life. Not only have we been sent out, but in our lives many of us have come close, at one time or another, to being "burnt out." So we draw near to Christ and to one another. As priest disciples of Jesus, we need *to be together,* we need *to pray together,* we need *to reflect together* on Jesus' mission and on our own mission—our own pastoral mission.

Let us allow ourselves once again to be captivated and inspired by the pastoral mission of Jesus. I would like to emphasize one aspect of the mission of Jesus—one aspect of His being the Good Shepherd. Our Gospel is magnificent in what it tells us about Jesus and about ourselves.

In the Gospel of Saint John, in chapter ten, Jesus Himself tells us *five times* what being the Good Shepherd is all about—for Himself and for us. Five times He speaks about offering His life—laying down His life for His sheep. *Laying down His life is the distinct act of the Good Shepherd.* It distinguishes Him from the hired hand. But there is another element in His laying down His life that is of capital importance. Jesus tells us that the Father loves Him, because He lays down His life: "This is why the Father loves me, because I lay down my life" (John 10:17).

The Father Loves Us As He Loves Jesus

Jesus is situating His pastoral role within the life of the Most Blessed Trinity. The Father loves Jesus, because Jesus takes care of the flock—because He lays down His life for the Church.

Jesus wants to make sure that we do not miss the point of His words. He insists that He lays down His life *freely:* "No one takes it from me, but I lay it down on my own. And then He repeats again: "I have power to lay it down, and power to take it up again" (John 10:18).

Those words of Jesus are His special gift to us. In earlier chapters of Saint John, Jesus tells us that the Father loves Him. Then, He tells us *why.* It is not the only reason, but it is a very special reason: because of His pastoral generosity—because He lays down His life freely for the flock.

I would hope for *one special grace* for all of us: *to realize that we are loved by the Father;* to realize that the same love that the Father has for Jesus, because He lays down His life for the flock, He also has for us His priests because, by His gift and grace, *we* lay down our life for the flock.

We Have the Power!

The fifth time Jesus uses the words "to lay down His life" He joins it with the phrase "I have the power." My dear brothers, we too have the power—the power to lay down our lives! We have already exercised it since the beginning of our priesthood—the way Jesus did.

Yes, it is a big challenge to lay down our lives repeatedly—every day—with total generosity, but we are trying. And the point is—the Father loves us just as He loves Jesus. This makes it all worthwhile. This brings it all into perspective. This gives us strength not to be afraid; to launch ourselves continually into the pastoral mission as it existed for Jesus and as it exists for us.

In the Consciousness of Being Loved!

Knowing that we are loved gives us new energy in the never-ending demands of our pastoral ministry. It also gives us new energy to reflect on those words of prophecy in the Book of Ezekiel that apply to Jesus and to ourselves: "I myself will pasture my sheep . . . The lost I will seek out, the strayed I will bring back, the injured I will bind up, the sick I will heal . . . shepherding them rightly" (Ezekiel 34:15–16).

All of this requires strength on our part—a strength that comes from the consciousness that we are loved by the Father, just as Jesus was. And being loved by the Father, we have the strength to love, to lay down our lives for the flock in pastoral love, and to continue seeking out those in need of our pastoral ministry—our pastoral love.

Remember, my brothers, like Jesus we have the power!

11

Ministry of Merciful Love

Dear brother Priests, dear Friends,

How important it is for you to have brother priests who show you the solidarity and fraternity of the priesthood! They are witnesses to you that your priestly ministry is not a personal possession, an individualistic exercise of good. Your priesthood, as they testify, is exercised in the unity of the presbyterate, with them, with your Bishop, with the Bishop of Rome, and with the whole Catholic Church.

You have received *the anointing of the Holy Spirit*. The prophecy of Isaiah has long since been fulfilled in Jesus, and it is also fulfilled in you: "The Spirit of the Lord is upon me . . . He has sent me to bring good tidings to the lowly, to heal the brokenhearted" (Isaiah 61:1). You are servants of God's word, and God's word proclaims His love and uplifts the world. You are sent into the world to tell again the story of God's love, to bear witness to this love, and to do this in a special way. You have been called to perform sacramental acts in the name of Jesus, in memory of Him. You are men of the Eucharist and the forgiveness of sins. You have been called to bring healing, comfort, and consolation to those in need. You have been called to serve the world with the bread of life and the word of God, to proclaim justice, to exercise mercy. And in everything you do, you strive to fulfill the command of Jesus: "Do this in memory of me" (Luke 22:19).

In his Letter to the Romans, Saint Paul has told you that there are many gifts in the Church. In particular, *the gift of ministry is to be used for service,* authority is to be exercised with care, and works of mercy are to be done cheerfully. All of this is part of the challenge that the Church places before you every day—a challenge that the grace of God empowers you to fulfill.

Through the power of God's word proclaimed in the liturgy and actuated in the Sacrament of Holy Orders, the encounter of the Apostles with the Risen Jesus is shared with you. It is to you in a very special way that Jesus Christ the Son of God says today and every day of your lives: "Peace be with you" (John 20:19). And He breathes on you and imparts to you the Spirit that He Himself possesses in fullness—the Spirit of God's love. Through the outpouring of this Spirit, Jesus transmitted to your custody *His Easter gift to His Church:* "Whose sins you forgive are forgiven them, and whose sins you retain are retained" (John 20:23).

Christ's Easter Gift

The Easter gift of Jesus Christ is *mercy.* It is manifested in the forgiveness of sins. Your priestly ministry engages you in the greatest attribute of God: *loving mercy.* You are forever instruments of God's forgiveness, His pardon, His compassion. You exist in order to proclaim the mercy of God, to perpetuate in the Church Christ's Easter gift of forgiveness.

The exercise of divine mercy is what Christ's life and your priesthood is all about. The Last Supper, Calvary,

Christ's Resurrection to new life, His Easter gift of the Sacrament of Penance or Reconciliation, the Eucharist, the Church—all this is the revelation of God's mercy *in the forgiveness of sins.*

In the very act of consecrating the Eucharist, which is the source and summit of your Christian and priestly lives, you will repeat the words of Jesus: "This is the cup of my blood, the blood of the new and everlasting covenant. It will be shed for you and for all *so that sins may be forgiven.* Do this in memory of me."

Dear brothers, your priestly ministry, which embraces Christ's Supper and Sacrifice and His Easter gift of pardon, *is a ministry of merciful love.* Everything you are and do must bear witness to merciful love. So that you may worthily exercise this ministry of mercy, Jesus today gives you His peace in the Holy Spirit. He gives you His Mother Mary to intercede for you with maternal love and He gives you the support of His holy Church. And remember that Jesus tells you, "As the Father has sent me, so I send you" (John 20:22).

12

The Love of Christ's Heart Explains Our Life

Dear brother Priests, dear Friends,

The solemnity of *the Sacred Heart* that we celebrate year after year is very important for all of us. It is *a special moment in the liturgical year* of the Church.

Since the beginning of the Church's year, we celebrate *so many different aspects of the mysteries of Christ.*

On the feast of the Annunciation we proclaim God's plan of *the Incarnation* of His Son—how the eternal Son of God took on our humanity in the womb of the Virgin Mary and became one of us.

In Advent we prepare for Christ's coming.

At Christmas we celebrate *the birth of Jesus* in Bethlehem. We adore the Child: true God and true man.

Then we reflect on the events of His hidden and public life, leading up to *His Paschal Mystery:* His Passion, Death, and Resurrection.

We prolong the celebration of Christ's Resurrection throughout Eastertime, rejoicing at the feast of *His Ascension* into heaven.

Then comes *Pentecost*—full of meaning for us: the sending of the Holy Spirit upon the Apostles, the beginning of the Church's mission with the temporal extension of the Incarnation in the Body of Christ.

After Pentecost, those beautiful feasts: the solemnity of *the Most Blessed Trinity* which speaks to us not only about the life of God but also about how the unity of the Church reflects the communion of the love of the Father and the Son in the Holy Spirit.

Then we celebrate *Corpus Christi:* the feast of the Body and Blood of Jesus Christ, which in the Eucharist becomes our food and drink.

Symbol of Love and Sign of Life

And finally, we have, the feast of the Sacred Heart of Jesus. It is the feast of *the Incarnate Word* of God, the Son of God, *manifesting His love for us* and *showing us His Heart as a sign of that love.* But the love that He shows us is none other than the love that He has received from His Father. Remember His words: "As the Father has loved me, so I also love you" (John 15:9).

The feast of the Sacred Heart therefore embraces the love of the Father—the One who so loved the world that He sent His only begotten Son into the world to redeem the world. With a human heart, Christ loves both *His Father* and all those who, through His Incarnation, have become *His brothers and sisters in humanity.*

The Heart that Christ shows us is His living human Heart—united to His living humanity. It is a symbol of His love. But even more it is *the sign of His life,* because the living Heart sustains His human life. And *in God, life and love are identical.*

The love that inspired the Son of God to become man is the same love that inspired Him to die so as to destroy our death, and to rise so as to restore us to life. The love of God explains why Christ came into the world, why He died and rose from the dead, why He set up the Church and sent the Holy Spirit—the Spirit of Love— to be with us forever.

The love of Christ's Heart explains the Eucharist, the living memorial of Christ's Passion, Death, and Resurrection. And what is also so clear for us is that *the love of Christ's Heart also explains the great gift and mystery of the priesthood.*

When Pope John Paul II went to St. Louis in 1999, he spoke about the merciful love of God that passes through the Heart of Jesus Christ. *The merciful love* of God that passes through the Heart of Jesus Christ is *the cause of the priesthood.* And the priesthood is given so that the gift and mystery of Christ's love can be perpetuated in a very special way in the Church.

A Specific Service of Love

The ministerial priesthood exists so that *a specific service of love* may be exercised in the Church. What is this specific service? It is *the celebration of the Eucharist* and the gathering of a community around an altar to praise God through Jesus Christ, the great High Priest. It is He, Jesus Christ, whom we represent and sacramentally make present.

Through the priesthood, the merciful love of God is also poured out *in the Sacrament of Penance,* through which Jesus Christ continues to forgive sins and to bring humanity into the merciful and compassionate embrace of His Father.

And in numerous other ways too, *we mediate the love of Christ to others* through our own humanity—as long as our human heart is able to sustain our human life.

Dear brothers, as priests of Jesus Christ, we are men of service, but our greatest service to the community is *to offer Mass for the living and the dead.* Vatican II teaches us that the pastoral love that priests have for the people "flows mainly from the Eucharistic Sacrifice which is therefore the center and root of the whole priestly life" (*Prebyterorum Ordinis,* 14).

The love of Jesus Christ explains His life and it is the reason for the Eucharistic Sacrifice. This love also explains our life. It is the reason we celebrate the Eucharist, the reason we give our life in priestly service and in consecrated celibacy.

Mary, the Mother of Jesus, supported the apostles by her maternal love. May she help us to understand and live *our vocation of priestly love,* which links us ever more closely to the love of God that passes through the Heart of Jesus.

13

Eternal Reward of Every Priest: The Word of God

Dear brother Priests, dear Friends,

All of us know that the priesthood is part of God's plan for the redemption of the world, as is the life and death of each individual priest.

To all of you, my brother priests, I express special gratitude for your priestly bond of solidarity and communion with the priests who have entered eternal life. *This bond is stronger than death,* because your faith and fraternal love are stronger than death, and the love of Jesus Christ that gave us all the gift of the priesthood is stronger than death.

Belonging Forever to Our Local Churches

We were all associated with our brother priests in different ways and in varying degrees of friendship and fraternity. They were all part of a presbyterate, and their priestly lives and ministries belong forever to the sacred history of salvation in our local Churches. We greet with deep affection the memory and the holy remembrances of their lives. We invoke God's loving mercy on their souls and ask for all of them the joy and peace of eternal life in the communion of the Most Blessed Trinity.

We are grateful to our deceased brothers for their faith, their long years of priestly service, their perseverance in their vocation.

One element that was so important in the life and ministry of each of our brother priests was *the living word of God.* It was the reason they, and we, were ordained priests: in order to proclaim God's word and to celebrate its supreme sacramental proclamation in the Sacrifice and Supper of Christ.

The word of God is a challenge to the ministry of each priest. He is called to be a faithful dispenser of God's revelation. But the Word of God is also *the reward of every priestly life.*

In the Communion of Saints

Our deceased brother priests can still rightly proclaim the message of Isaiah the Prophet: "Behold our God, to whom we looked to save us! This is the Lord for whom we looked; let us rejoice and be glad that he has saved us" (Isaiah 25:9). In the Communion of Saints we join with our brothers in thanking God through Jesus Christ for the salvation they have already obtained, or in beseeching Him for any purification that still may be necessary for them.

How appropriate it is that we commemorate their going forth from us by recalling the Gospel that they preached. Saint Paul tells us—and our brothers repeated this frequently: "Remember Jesus Christ, raised from the dead, a descendant of David: such is my gospel" (2 Timothy 2:8–9). And he continues: "If we have died with him, we shall also live with him; if we persevere, we shall also reign with him" (v. 11).

Yes, dear friends, we give thanks for the perseverance of our priests, notwithstanding human weaknesses and difficulties, and we are convinced that God's promise is being fulfilled in the *gift of everlasting life.*

So much of their ministry, so much of their daily lives was in *the Eucharist.* They proclaimed Christ's promise of giving us His body and His blood. They wholeheartedly accepted and believed the words of Jesus that eternal life is the gift that the Eucharist brings, and they faithfully celebrated the Eucharist, receiving the Lord's body and blood, waiting in joyful hope for the coming of our Savior Jesus Christ.

The words of Jesus in the Gospel affirm that their faith, hope, and love were not in vain. Jesus solemnly assures us: "Whoever eats my flesh and drinks my blood has eternal life, and I will raise him up on the last day." The reason, Jesus says, is: "For my flesh is true food and my blood is true drink" (John 6:53–55).

Every time we commemorate the death of our brother priests, we renew our own holy, Catholic, and apostolic faith, as we look for *the resurrection of the dead and the life of the world to come.*

Commitment for the Life of the World

In the tragedy in New York on September 11, 2001, a priest gave his life for his people. His death was claimed—and rightly so—as an act of great generosity and priestly love.

The death of most of our priests is not so dramatic, but it is no less valuable for the Church, no less precious in the eyes of God. For each of them death represented their *final configuration to the death of Jesus Christ,* in anticipation of their sharing in His Resurrection.

Even as we pray for them, we are mindful of the opportunity their death gives us to do three things:

1. To experience, in depth, communion with them;

2. To proclaim our faith in the Resurrection of Jesus Christ from the dead;

3. To recommit ourselves to our priestly Eucharistic ministry, in the profound assurance that "If anyone eats this bread, he shall live forever."

Number 1: *Our communion* with our deceased brother priests *is deeper than ever.* We believe that they are destined for the fullness of eternal life in heaven. If necessary, they pass through the great purifying and merciful love of Jesus Christ—still obtainable after death, known as *Purgatory.* In either case, we are still in union with our brothers. We offer prayers for their souls, knowing that eventually, if not already, they will be our intercessors in heaven.

They have shared our life, our troubles, our joys, our challenges. They have gone before us with the sign of faith. Nothing can separate us—fellow Christians, fellow participants in the priesthood of Christ—from *our common destiny in the Communion of Saints.* Our brothers encourage us in the words of the prophet Isaiah: "Behold our God, to whom we looked to save us! This is the Lord for whom we looked; let us rejoice and be glad that he has saved us" (Isaiah 25:9).

Number 2: To celebrate Mass for our deceased brothers is a magnificent occasion for us to proclaim our faith, our holy Catholic faith, in the Resurrection of Jesus Christ. We have heard Saint Paul say to us, "Remember Jesus Christ, raised from the dead, a descendant of David." And he went on to say, "If we have died with him, we shall also live with him" (2 Timothy 2:8, 11).

Paul's faith is our faith and proclamation, and the faith and proclamation of the Church. How privileged we are, dear brother priests, to be able *to proclaim* to our people *Jesus Christ crucified and risen from the dead,* Jesus Christ, the cause of our resurrection and eternal life!

Number 3: In remembering our deceased brother priests we recommit ourselves to our priestly Eucharistic ministry.

From our youth we have heard Jesus speaking to us in the Gospel, saying, "I am the living bread. . . . Whoever eats this bread will live forever; and the bread that I will give is my flesh for the life of the world" (John 6:51).

By God's grace we were attracted to the Eucharist and began to understand its meaning in our lives. And then we realized *our Eucharistic vocation to the priesthood* and to the celebration of the Eucharist as the bread of life for our people. And we came to know, in the faith of the Church, that the Eucharist is offered for the living and the dead.

When we offer the Eucharist for the dead, and in particular for our deceased brothers, *we recommit ourselves to this Eucharistic ministry of ours.* We remember, we celebrate, we believe.

We *remember* the words of Jesus: "Whoever eats my flesh and drinks my blood has eternal life and I will raise him on the last day" (John 6:54). *We celebrate* this promise of eternal life, and *we believe* that the one who feeds on this bread shall live forever.

In communion with our deceased brother priests and all the faithful departed, we renew our Eucharistic priestly commitment to the Church for the life of the world.

14

Our Young Priest Brothers

Dear brother Priests, dear Friends,

It is always a day of profound joy for the presbyterate when our priests, with fraternal love, welcome into their company new brothers in the partnership of the Gospel.

Scripture draws our attention to the person of Jesus Christ, High Priest and Good Shepherd of the Church. It presents Him as the one who proclaims the good news of God's kingdom, the one who is concerned for every sickness and disease, and the one whose Heart is moved with compassion at seeing the crowds like sheep without a shepherd.

We Welcome Our Young Priests

In this context of the word of God, we celebrate the special calling of young men configured to Christ as High Priest and Good Shepherd of His people. They are chosen just as we were, for a special pastoral role as priests of Jesus Christ.

They are part of our families, many of them have come from our local Church, and they are all called to serve our local Church.

Just like Jesus, their role is to proclaim the good news of salvation. For this they are ordained through the laying on of hands and the invocation of the Holy Spirit. They are called to join their Bishop and their fellow priests in transmitting the apostolic message. In the presbyterate they are linked to the College of Bishops. As a result, like Peter they can say: "He—Jesus—commissioned us to preach" (Acts 10:42).

Sacramental Witnesses

According to the teaching and life of the Church, this preaching or proclamation is done by word and example and signs. This proclamation reaches its culmination in the Eucharistic signs of bread and wine, which become the sacramental proclamation of Christ's death and resurrection.

And so our young priests become sacramental witnesses to the love of God as shown in the death and resurrection of Christ.

The greatest role of service of all priests is the Eucharist. Through it we bring redemption to humanity. We bring Jesus the Redeemer to His people.

Another absolutely essential role of the servant priest is the forgiveness of sins. He is the one to whom Christ entrusts His work of mercy and compassion, His own ministry or reconciliation.

Who then is the priest? Who is our young priest brother?

- He is the one who with us offers the Eucharistic Sacrifice.
- The one who forgives sins.
- The one who proclaims Jesus Christ as the High Priest and Good Shepherd of the Church.
- He is the one who, like Christ, lays down his life to build up the community of the Church in faith and love,

giving it the word of God, offering to it the hope and joy promised by Jesus Christ.

Our Brothers and Our Friends

Our young priests are our brothers and our friends: the ones who have most recently responded generously to the call of Christ. The ones who presented themselves with only one ambition: to serve and serve and serve God's people to the end. To serve as the Church calls them to serve: humbly, generously, chastely, with joy, giving of themselves but transmitting always the word of God as proclaimed by the Catholic Church.

They are the ones who have accepted to do all this, not by their own strength but by the power of God's Spirit, and they have accepted to do this as part of the community. They have thrown in their lot with that of Christ and His people. And so, they are a living, loving part of God's people. They share their lives with their people, never losing sight that their people belong to Christ.

They want to share their people's joys and sorrows, their hopes, their anxieties, their longing for eternal life— but they want to share all this from within the community.

They pray with our people, and our people pray with them. They understand our people—their strengths and weaknesses—just as our people understand them.

As part of a long line of faithful priests, they love our people in the charity of Christ, and in this love they challenge our people—just as the people challenge them— to live the Gospel fully, even beyond the measure of human weakness, by the grace of Jesus Christ.

They are with our people in times of gladness and trial:

- for Baptisms, for marriages, in sickness, at death;
- to offer the Eucharistic Sacrifice with their community for the living and the dead;
- to counsel and encourage;
- to be heralds of justice and servants of truth;
- and to forgive in the name of Jesus and through His mercy and His power.

The Next Generation

As our new priests endeavor to lay down their lives for all their brothers and sisters, their hearts long particularly to help other young men reach the priesthood. They can never forget hearing the Gospel that described Christ's heart being moved by compassion as He told His disciples, "The harvest is abundant, but the laborers are few; so ask the master of the harvest to send out laborers for his harvest" (Luke 10:2).

Our young priests are indeed called to work and pray and strive to attract other disciples by the joy and sacrifice and fervor of their priestly lives.

The Church is proud of the grace of Jesus Christ that repeatedly brings new priests among us. She is likewise deeply grateful for their generosity in saying *yes* to the call of the Lord. As parents, families, friends, and brother priests surround our young priests in prayerful solidarity and loving support, the words of the Apostle Paul challenge us all in the name of Jesus. "I urge you," he says, "to live in a manner worthy of the calling you have received, with all humility and gentleness, with patience, bearing with one another through love, striving to preserve the unity of the Spirit through the bond of peace" (Ephesians 4:1–2).

We welcome our young brothers and friends to the priesthood of Jesus Christ, to the presbyterate, to a ministry of service that comes from Christ, belongs to Christ, and leads to Christ.

As we priests strive to serve God's people, we know too that Mary, the Mother of Jesus, who has become Mother of His Church, accompanies all His priests with her prayers and intercessions and maternal love.

May Mary sustain us all to the end in joy and charity, in fidelity and chastity, in generous service to God's people for the glory of the Most Blessed Trinity: Father, Son and Holy Spirit.

15

We Need the Eucharist,
We Need Priests

Dear brother Priests, dear Friends,

We reflect on the meaning of the life and death of our priests, to express our solidarity in the communion of saints with those *who have gone before us*. We pray for them and express *our unbreakable confidence that their sacred ministry will be carried on in the Church,* that the power of Christ's Paschal Mystery will raise up generous young men in this generation to perpetuate their priestly work.

We are especially *grateful* to God for the life and death of our priests, for their fidelity in carrying on the ministry of Jesus in the Church. They were above all ministers of the Eucharist. *They proclaimed the mystery of the Body and Blood of Christ.*

They themselves ate the bread of life, the Body of the Lord offered up in sacrifice; they drank His Blood. They were thus recipients of His wonderful promise: "Whoever eats my flesh and drinks my blood has eternal life and I will raise him on the last day" (John 6:54). *We proclaim their reward,* because Jesus has assured us that the man who eats this bread shall live forever.

Our brother priests were first and foremost baptized Christians, disciples of the Lord Jesus, but they were called to be ministers of His Church. In God's plan, *the bread of life comes to the whole Church only through the ministry of priests.* They themselves were sons of God; they had received the Spirit of adoption. They were also priests whose special ministry called for deep intimacy with Jesus. Through Jesus they were in daily contact with the Father and were able to call Him "Abba"—a term of intimacy and endearment.

Bringing the Living Jesus Christ to Our People

As priests, they were the channels and instruments of grace for all the people of God. No Christian who ever lived in the twenty centuries of our Church has ever shared in the Eucharist independently of the ministry of the priest.

For countless years of priestly service, these deceased brothers of ours, through the Eucharist, brought the living Jesus Christ to our people. *Their lives were deeply meaningful and sacred* because through them the whole community could eat the flesh and drink the blood of the Son of God.

These are the priests—our priests, our brothers. Human? Yes. Imperfect? Yes. But all of them were tried and purified in the *experience of suffering.* And each one of them could say with Saint Paul: "I consider that the sufferings of the present time are as nothing compared with the glory to be revealed for us" (Romans 8:13).

We bless the memory of all the priests of Jesus Christ. We boast of our solidarity with them in the Communion of Saints.

We likewise pray for them. Just as they were ordained to offer sacrifice for the living and the dead, so now we offer up this sacrifice of praise for them.

Their time has come and gone. Every priest knows that he receives a sacred trust. The Holy Spirit breathes where He wills—in and outside the structures of the Church. He accomplishes marvels of grace in every way He deems fit. But once Christ established the priesthood and the Eucharist, the only means to receive the Body and Blood of Christ is through the priestly ministry. The priest alone—because God has willed it so—acting in the name and person of Jesus Christ, can consecrate the Eucharist and, with it, give to all the people of God the gift of everlasting life. Jesus said, "Whoever eats my flesh and drinks my blood has eternal life" (John 6:54).

Our brother priests, while guiding and leading and serving the people of God, in every facet of their human existence, were ministers to them of eternal life. As we commemorate their service, their lives, and their contribution to the Church, *we profess our faith in the priesthood* just as Christ founded it—linked as it is forever to the Eucharist and the other sacraments of Christ's mercy, especially the Sacrament of Penance.

In Every Generation

Every priest knows how important his ministry is, how Christ calls him to make a wonderful contribution to the Church—but it is *only for a season*. The individual priest, Bishop or Pope can minister only for a season and then Christ calls new disciples in each generation to carry on His Eucharist, to carry on His Church, to lead His people to eternal life.

As we profess our Catholic faith in the priesthood, as we commemorate our faithful brothers who shared the joys and burdens of this sacred office, we unhesitatingly profess our confidence in Christ, *the divine Master of His Church in every generation.*

We are confident, fully confident, that the words spoken in the Book of the Prophet Jeremiah will be fulfilled. God promises His people "a future full of hope" (Jeremiah 29:11). We trust that the power of Christ's grace in future generations of His priests will indeed ensure this "future full of hope."

The power of the Paschal Mystery remains forever operative in the Eucharist. *Christ is able to attract to Himself— today as ever before—generous young men* to carry on the mystery of the Eucharist.

Our brother priests whom we joyfully commemorate have died, knowing that the Lord will raise up sufficient successors to them. Yes, there is a condition: The Church must work and pray and faithfully celebrate the Eucharist. But the Church must trust and speak about vocations to the priesthood, and about the joy and fulfillment that there is in living and dying so that the bread of life may be given to all the faithful.

We are grateful to you, our brother priests who have gone before us, for your dedicated lives and *for your Eucharistic faith.* We thank you for persevering in your vocation to be Eucharistic servants of God's people. We thank you for celebrating Mass for the living and the dead, for reminding the faithful how *the Eucharist is the source and summit of their Christian lives,* and how it also constitutes the challenge of their relationship to others, for proclaiming how *authentic participation in the Eucharist requires humble and generous service to our neighbor.* We thank you for professing *the real presence of Christ in the Eucharist.* We thank you for every hour you ever spent before the Blessed Sacrament praying for your people, for the Church.

We thank you for your generous response to the call of Christ to bring the Bread of eternal life to the local Church. As we recall your sacred memory, we entrust you all to the *prayers of Mary,* Mother of Priests and Queen of heaven.

16

Do You Realize What He Has Done for You?

Dear brother Priests, dear Friends,

On Holy Thursday, the texts of Sacred Scripture immerse us in the mystery of the Eucharist. To understand the liturgy that we celebrate we must speak about the Eucharist itself, about the priesthood, without which the Eucharist cannot exist, and about Christ's commandment of love and service. Jesus says, "I give you a new commandment: love one another. As I have loved you . . ." (John 13:34).

Holy Thursday is the anniversary of *the institution of the Eucharist*. It is also the anniversary of *the institution of the priesthood*. The two sacraments go together. There can be no Eucharist without the priesthood. The priesthood exists to make the Eucharist possible.

Christ's Attitude of Love and Service

Saint John does not speak about the Eucharist. The other three evangelists—Matthew, Mark, and Luke—describe its institution. Saint Paul does so also. Saint John, on the other hand, presumes it and goes on to speak about *Christ's attitude of love and service*, which was the reason Christ instituted the Eucharist and the priesthood.

These then are the three elements that make up any Holy Thursday reflection: 1) the gift of the Eucharist, 2) the gift of the priesthood, and 3) Christ's love for us manifested in washing the feet of his apostles in humble service.

The institution of the Eucharist is beautifully described for us by Saint Paul in his Letter to the Corinthians. This Letter was written only about twenty years after the death and resurrection of Jesus. This is the first account of what took place at the Last Supper. It precedes the accounts written by Matthew, Mark, and Luke.

The words that Saint Paul records are the basic formula that you pronounce in every Eucharist: "This is my body which will be given up for you." "This is the cup of my blood. . . . It will be shed for you. . . ." And finally: "Do this in memory of me."

Christ's command—"Do this in memory of me"—links the Eucharist and your priesthood. The Church teaches that *the Apostles* whom Jesus had chosen to celebrate the Eucharist *passed on this power* to their successors in the priesthood.

Again and Again

What is it that you are doing in memory of Christ?

The Church *evokes the memory* of Christ's Last Supper, but she does this in a sacramental way. She makes this Supper sacramentally present for us.

We know also that this Last Supper was the proclamation—as Saint Paul says—of the death of the Lord. The Last Supper was itself *the anticipation of the Sacrifice* that Christ would consummate on Good Friday by His death on the Cross.

And so the Church teaches that each of our Eucharistic celebrations, each of our Masses, is *the sacramental re-enactment of the death of Jesus.* The Eucharist brings us into contact with the Redemption that Jesus accomplished by His death and resurrection.

The Eucharist again and again sacramentally re-presents the Last Supper. It re-presents again and again the Sacrifice of Calvary. It makes actual in our lives the liberating action that Jesus accomplished by his death and resurrection.

For us, every Holy Thursday means *the Mass* and *the priest* who celebrates every Mass: our Lord Jesus Christ Himself. Holy Thursday also means *the love that motivated Jesus* to gather His apostles together at the Last Supper and to die for them, and for all of us, on Good Friday.

The Challenge of Surrender

Holy Thursday means for us *the challenge to follow Jesus* in the loving service that He performs for His apostles by washing their feet. Jesus was willing to serve others generously. He was willing to give His life in sacrifice for the redemption of the world.

Jesus gives us the privilege of celebrating His Eucharist, which is both Sacrifice and Supper. He also challenges us to *embrace His sentiments,* to take on His attitude, to love one another as He has loved us, to be willing to surrender ourselves in service to one another.

"Do you realize what I have done for you?"—Jesus says to us. "You call me 'teacher' and 'master,' and rightly so, for indeed I am" (John 13:12–13).

In the Gospel we read those words about Jesus that "He loved his own in the world and he loved them to the end" (John 13:1).

It was in the context of this love that, at the Last
Supper, Jesus took off His cloak, knelt down, and washed
the feet of His disciples. The Church continues this
ritual in our Holy Thursday Mass of the Lord's Supper, but
the Church is very eager for us to understand the deepest
meaning of this gesture.

His Love Gave You the Gift of Your Priesthood

This gesture of loving service to His disciples was
an expression of Christ's love for them. He found a gesture
that would express that love in an act of service, and at the
same time would challenge all generations of priests to find
every act of service possible to express their love, the love
that they had learned from Him, their love for one another.

At the core of every Holy Thursday celebration
is *the love of Jesus:* the love *that inspired Him to give us the
Eucharist, the love that urged Jesus to give you the gift of
your priesthood,* the love of Jesus that wanted to express itself
in the humble service of *kneeling before His disciples in order
to teach* them by His example how they were to act.

Christ has left this gesture also as *an incentive to
the creativity of the Church* so that throughout the centuries
the Church will find every means possible to convey the
love that Christ had in His heart for His people. The Church
will always remember that Jesus said, "Love one another
as I love you" (John 15:12).

The love of Christ urges you on, first to recognize
His love, to proclaim His gift of the Eucharist and
your priesthood then to find every creative means possible
to serve one another in the love that comes from His heart.
This love is a love that brings peace. And because we are
a Eucharistic people, we are challenged to be peacemakers

in all our work, in our mission, in our parishes, and in our various communities. To celebrate and receive the Eucharist means that we are called to pray and work for peace in the world—for the peace of Christ.

17

The Triumph of the Cross

Dear brother Priests, dear Friends,

At the invitation of our Holy Father Pope John Paul II we are privileged to celebrate *the Day of Sanctification for Priests* every year.

A very important aspect of our celebration is that we are in solidarity with the priests of the world. A very appropriate day for our celebrations is the feast of the Holy Cross because it is particularly meaningful to our Lord Jesus Christ Himself. It represents His triumph, the triumph of His work, His work for the Church.

Something extremely significant about the life of Christ is that *He is not alone.* In the Gospels Christ tells us this explicitly. He experiences deep communion with His Father, and He proclaims this, saying, "The one who has sent me is with me; he has not left me alone . . ." (John 8:29). On another occasion He says, "I am not alone, because the Father is with me" (John 16:32). Christ's consciousness of being one with His Father pervades His life and His mission. It is a source of strength for Him. Even at the height of His Passion, He knows that He is not abandoned, even though He suffers in His human nature the anguish of loneliness.

This also means that we are not alone. We can never be alone. We are not alone in our paschal struggles, in our weaknesses, in our anxieties, our joys, our pastoral concerns (and how many there are!), in our fragile sinful condition, in our Christian hopes, in our condition of being loved by Christ, in our discipleship, and in our call to holiness. *We are not alone.*

Our call to holiness is *a call to be like Christ*—a call to be *whole* and *new,* and yet to coexist between the weakness of our human condition—it is actually our glory!—and the strength of Christ. It is our call to be constantly converted in Christ the Man, Christ the Priest, Christ the Son of the eternal Father.

In the Context of Faith and Love

The Scriptures speak powerfully to us and to our priesthood. We find the Israelites on a journey out of bondage through the desert on to freedom. They are still in the midst of suffering and difficulties, suffering from their own sins. In their condition of sinfulness they needed relief from the serpents that were attacking them. Through Moses, God gave them the bronze serpent mounted on a pole. As they looked up and gazed upon this bronze serpent —a type of Christ lifted up on the Cross—they were healed in anticipation of the power—in anticipation of the Triumph—of the Cross.

Jesus personally compares Himself and His saving work to what was accomplished through the instrumentality of the bronze serpent. And He puts it in the context of faith: "Just as Moses lifted up the serpent in the desert, so must the Son of Man be lifted up, that everyone who believes in him may have eternal life" (John 3:14–15). God so loved the world that He gave His only Son so that everyone who believes in Him may not perish but might have eternal life. For God did not send the Son into the world to condemn the world, but that the world might be saved through Him" (John 3:16–17).

Here we can pinpoint the Triumph of the Cross: Humanity looks up to Jesus on the Cross and receives from Him the gift of the Father's love, which is eternal life.

Here we can also pinpoint our priesthood: our instrumental sharing in the saving action of Christ accomplished on the Cross, even as we ourselves are saved, looking up to the One who assumed our humanity, took on all our weaknesses and even—in the expression of Saint Paul—became sin for us, "He made him to be sin" (2 Corinthians 5:21).

In the Letter to the Philippians, Saint Paul spells out explicitly the meaning of Christ's Triumph on the Cross: "Because of this," he says, "God greatly exalted Him and bestowed on Him the name that is above every name, that at the name of Jesus . . . every tongue [must] confess that Jesus Christ is Lord to the glory of the Father" (Philippians 2:9–10).

With these words we are brought back to *the meaning of the Day of Sanctification for Priests.*

Renewed Hope and Trust

We are invited *to proclaim by the authenticity of our priestly lives that Jesus Christ is Lord.* We are invited to proclaim by our renewed commitment—our renewed commitment to prayer and humble service, to the Eucharist, to the Sacrament of Penance, to the teaching of the Apostles, to the *communion* of the Church—that Jesus Christ is Lord. It is so important that we do this together, realizing that, like Jesus, *we are not alone.* For we are privileged, like

Jesus, to live with the Father in the communion of the Holy Spirit. We have the unity of our presbyterate, the unity of priestly brotherhood throughout the world.

We experience a special strength to pursue our vocation to holiness because we know of *the support of our people.* Thousands of the faithful sustain us in prayer. As they do this, they also offer us the example of their Christian struggle, their generous daily lives, their love for the Church, their joy in living the mystery of the Cross, and their faith in the Triumph of the Cross through the Resurrection and in eternal life. Cloistered nuns intercede for us. Many of the sick offer up their suffering for us.

Our people are aware that *our fidelity* to Christ's call to conversion and holiness of life has a great impact on our ministry, on all the services we render in the name of Christ.

In the midst of this tremendous solidarity, this wonderful communion of faith and love which we live with our people, *let us renew our hope* and our trust in the power of Christ's Cross, in the Triumph of Christ's Cross.

The universal Church proclaims this Triumph every day. It is Christ's Triumph over sins and weaknesses— our sins and our weaknesses—over innumerable obstacles to the spread of His Gospel.

Do We Really Believe?

All of us are invited to look up to Christ with faith and trust, and in His Cross to find healing, holiness, and strength. Jesus speaks to us as He spoke in the Gospels: "Do you believe that I can do this?" (Matthew 9:28). To say *yes* is to acknowledge the Triumph of the Cross and to proclaim Jesus Christ as Lord.

Yes, we believe in Christ's healing and sanctifying power. It is operative not only in the abstract, but in us.

We believe that the power of *Christ's Paschal Mystery of death and resurrection* is indeed the *source of vocations to the priesthood* in every age of the Church and that Christ is still able in our own time to inspire young men to accept generously His call to the priesthood.

The Triumph of the Cross spurs us on to overcome discouragement, to re-evaluate the meaning of personal or pastoral setbacks, to reject all pessimism, and to plan courageously for the future of our local Church.

Meanwhile, dear brother priests, we continue our journey in our human condition, but under the sign of the Cross, *under the sign of the Triumph of the Cross.*

In the words of Saint Paul: "We have set our hope on the living God" (1 Timothy 4:10). In the Triumph of the Cross we proclaim that *Jesus Christ* is Lord!

We are not alone as Jesus was not alone. The Father was with Him. Mary His Mother was with Him in the suffering of the cross and in the joy of His Resurrection.

With *Christ and Mary* we have the communion of the Most Blessed Trinity. And we have each other, the love and support of one another—friends and brother priests in Jesus Christ.

18

Faith in the Loving Mercy of Our High Priest

Dear brother Priests, dear Friends,

It is a privilege for us *to celebrate Christian death,* and in particular the death of our brother priests.

In celebrating Christian death, we are celebrating *the triumph of Jesus over death.* He is victorious not only in theory, but in practice. He is victorious in those whom we have known and loved. He is the cause of their resurrection to eternal life. And so with Saint Paul we say, "Thanks be to God who gives us the victory through our Lord Jesus Christ" (1 Corinthians 15:57).

We proclaim *the power of faith* in Christ and in His word to make us pass from death to life. We recall the words of Jesus who tells us, "Whoever hears my word and believes in the one who sent me has eternal life and will not come to condemnation, but has passed from death to life" (John 5:24).

We proclaim that *Christ is stronger than death,* that by dying He has destroyed our death and by rising He has restored our life.

As priests we preach the word, but we also pause *to bear witness to what we preach.* We believe that our priest brothers heard Christ's word and believed in the one who sent Him. We believe that they have passed from death to life.

We know that *final purification* may still be necessary for them before their final contact with the holiness of God, and so we pray for our beloved dead. The Church leads us in this prayer and in its greatest expression, which is the Eucharistic sacrifice.

As priests we proclaim our faith in Christ our Savior, in the power that faith has to lead us to eternal life, in *the power of Christ's resurrection* to raise us up.

Final Purification: Gift of God's Mercy

We also proclaim our faith in a stupendous aspect of Christ's mercy, an incredible gift of His love. We reaffirm *the teaching of the Church on Purgatory*. When we pray for the dead, we implicitly acknowledge their possible need for help. We do more however than just acknowledge this need. Our God who is rich in mercy has devised a means to extend mercy even after death. The period of our human life closes with death; our fundamental option is definitely sealed with death—and yet God's mercy is without end. *The purification of our souls is still possible because of the dispensation of God's mercy* that passes through the Heart of Christ and allows yet another opportunity for us to be fully immersed in the mystery of salvific love. This is what the Church means by Purgatory.

This explains why we pray for our brother priests and for all our brothers and sisters who have gone before us with the sign of faith. We commend them, if such is still necessary, to the loving mercy of the great High Priest.

There is still even more to our faith: We proclaim the resurrection of the body and await its fulfillment. Christ is the first fruits of those who have fallen asleep. Also, Mary our Mother has already been glorified in her body. We who remain know that this destiny awaits us too.

The Commemoration of All the Faithful Departed, the feast of All Souls, is an appeal to all of us who make up the Church to proclaim the great mystery of the mercy of God—mercy that reveals itself in pardon, forgiveness, and eternal rest. The final purification of our beloved dead is linked to our prayers and to the Eucharistic sacrifice that we offer today and always as we invoke the mercy of God.

We are filled with hope. *The mystery of death reveals the mystery of God's mercy* that passes through the Heart of Christ. "Thanks be to God who gives us the victory through our Lord Jesus Christ" (1 Corinthians 15:57).

Death Is Our Friend

Some years ago, with the help of the media, Cardinal Bernardin of Chicago communicated to the nation the serious condition of his health and the announcement of his impending death. As a man of faith, he spoke of embracing death as a friend.

But in what sense is the great and radical separation that is death able to be called a friend?

Only because it is linked to the victorious death of Jesus—the Jesus who died and was raised up, who is at the right hand of God and who intercedes for us, as Saint Paul bears witness and as the Church proclaims.

Death links us to the Lamb who was slain, to the Victor who conquered death, to the One who lives triumphantly. Our death—when freely accepted—links us to the One who fulfills the promise of the Lord God, as we hear from the prophet Isaiah: "He will destroy death forever. The Lord God will wipe away the tears from all faces" (Isaiah 25:3).

Death is our friend because it links us irrevocably with the mystery of Christ's death and resurrection, which is the center of all Christian living and which constitutes the core of our priesthood, which we renew in the Eucharist. The Eucharist is the main reason for which we were ordained.

Death then, despite its pain, violence, and suffering, is that wonderful access to the company of Jesus. It is the means whereby Jesus' prayer is fulfilled to have His disciples near Him and with Him forever:

> Father,
> they are your gift to me.
> I wish that where I am
> they also may be with me,
> that they may see my glory
> that you gave me because you loved me
> before the foundation of the world.
> (John 17:24)

For Jesus, death was the moment of opportunity; for Him, it meant obedience to His Father's will, loving acceptance of His Father's plan. It meant the opportunity to show the depth of His love for His people. "He loved his own in the world," says Saint John, "and he loved them to the end" (John 13:1).

Death was the opportunity for Jesus to redeem His Mother, His disciples, all humanity. It was a great opportunity for Jesus to say *yes* to His Father—in the name of all His brothers and sisters—to make up for the *no* of Adam and for the *no* inherent in every actual sin committed in the course of history.

To Say *Yes* to God's Love

And so death—the death of a Christian, the death of a priest, is a wonderful way to say yes to God's love, to say *yes* to God's plan for us to share in Christ's redeeming and redemptive death.

The death of a priest is the final moment to say *yes* definitively to God, to reverse all the times we said *no* out of human weakness and sin, to ratify freely and decisively the gift of Baptism and the priesthood, and to consecrate forever our freedom to the Lord.

Even when death comes suddenly and unexpectedly, it has such power and efficacy because it will have been rehearsed a thousand times, not necessarily in its particular details, but by a personal and free act of obedience and surrender, in union with Christ, to the Father. We remember those last words of Jesus: "Father, unto your hands I commend my spirit" (Luke 23:46).

As we recall with gratitude and love our deceased brothers in the priesthood, we praise God for uniting their death to the death of Jesus. We thank God for their death, through which, with Jesus, they were invested with the power of His resurrection. And we praise God—Father, Son, and Holy Spirit—for giving us an understanding that our own death is a moment of exhilarating freedom, through which we consummate our own sacrificial love and open ourselves to eternal life in Jesus Christ, together with Mary and all the Saints.

19

God's Greatest Work in Us

Dear brother Priests, dear Friends,

I wish to tell you how very *grateful* I am to all of you, my brother priests, for promoting the unity of our priesthood, for responding to Pope John Paul II's invitation *to pray for the gift of holiness* for ourselves and our brother priests. We pray confidently knowing that God is with us, that He wills our holiness, and that His grace is able to accomplish in us far more than we can ask or imagine (cf. Ephesians 3:20). In our pursuit of holiness, *our mutual support is essential.*

Jesus Christ, as a Priest, offered to the Father the sacrifice of His life on the Cross. Today we are reflecting on the Cross as *the triumph of our great High Priest.*

The Cross is first of all *a personal triumph for Jesus.* He has done everything that the Father wanted Him to do. He assumed humanity from the Virgin Mary and became one of us. He submitted His humanity to the Father's plan by embracing the Cross. Saint Paul says: ". . . he humbled himself, becoming obedient to death, even death on a cross!" (Philippians 2:8) Because of this the Father glorified Jesus and constituted Him *as Lord.*

Before being constituted as Lord, Jesus is revealed, however, *as our Savior.* We see this so beautifully in the Gospel. Jesus Himself says: "God did not send the Son into the world to condemn the world but that the world might be saved through him" (John 3:17). Jesus compares Himself to the bronze serpent that was the instrument of God's forgiveness and mercy and healing in the Old Testament: "Just as Moses lifted up the serpent in the desert so must the Son of Man be lifted up, so that everyone who believes in him may have eternal life" (John 3:14–15).

Salvation Triumphs on the Cross

We look to Christ as the one who through His Cross saves us and brings us to eternal life. We are grateful that *salvation triumphed on the Cross* and through the Cross has reached us.

We praise God that *Jesus' work of salvation on the Cross was ratified and accepted by the Father,* who raised Jesus from the dead.

We praise God that Jesus' lasting triumph is summarized in His glorious title, Lord. Because He saved us on the Cross, "Jesus Christ is Lord!"

This brings us, dear brother priests, to a consideration of our own ministry as *collaborators of Christ in bringing His salvation to the world,* in bringing the triumph of the Cross into the hearts of our people. We have the opportunity to reflect on how privileged we are to work "to ensure that the power of salvation may be shared by all" (Pope John Paul II, *Tertio Millennio Adveniente,* 16). We do this through the Eucharist that we celebrate, through the Sacrament of Penance that we administer and receive, and in so many other ways—in prayer and celibacy, in joy and suffering, in patience, endurance, and hard work.

Do Not Forget the Works of the Lord!

We also have the special opportunity to heed the words of the psalmist as they apply to our own lives: *"Do not forget the works of the Lord!"* You and I have received so much from the Lord; we have been blessed in so many ways. One of these is *the outpouring of God's mercy in our lives!* The Father's love that passes through the heart of Jesus plus our weaknesses, plus our sins, equals divine mercy. *Mercy is God's love in the face of our sinfulness.* Mercy is God's greatest work in us. Mercy is the cause of our conversion and our perseverance.

The *triumph of the Cross,* which is a personal triumph for Jesus, *means forgiveness and pardon and mercy for us.* When we are told "Do not forget the works of the Lord!" we are being told not to forget His greatest work in our lives: His mercy—the mercy that manifests itself in the forgiveness of our sins. The psalmist further tells us today: "Yet he who is full of compassion forgave their sin and spared them. So often he held back his anger when he might have stirred up his rage" (Psalm 78:38).

Dear brother priests, "Do not forget the works of the Lord!" Let us not forget His mercy in our lives! *The triumph of the Cross brings us divine mercy,* and divine mercy is the power of salvation for us and for our people.

The triumph of the Cross is *an invitation* to each of us *to trust in the mercy of Jesus,* our High Priest, our Savior, our Lord.

20

Lord, Make Us Holy Men

Dear brother Priests, dear Friends,

Each of you is so important in accomplishing Christ's work in the Church. Because this is true, your sanctification as priests is so necessary.

Some time ago I was with a group of priests. One of them led a prayer in these words: "Lord, make us holy men. Lord, make us holy priests." My brothers, that is what we seek: to pray for holiness, so that we can fulfill worthily our Christian discipleship and our priestly life and ministry.

All of us know by intuition and experience that the success of our priestly ministry is linked, in God's plan, to our holiness of life.

So we pray for this intention: Lord, make us holy men. Lord, make us holy priests. We pray together. We pray with confidence. We pray in union with Christ, relying on the prayers of our Blessed Mother and the prayers of our parishioners, all our people. There is a lot at stake. Our two great intercessors are, in the words of Saint Paul, the Lord Jesus and His Holy Spirit.

We have every reason, then, to be joyful, to be confident, to be at peace.

In the Midst of the Mystery of Evil

We have in our times a different world, deeply touched by the mystery of iniquity, the mystery of evil.

This is the world in which we exercise our priestly ministry, the world we serve, the world we must evangelize, the world in which we are called to be heralds of hope. The evil is great, but our hope is strong because Jesus Christ is the same yesterday, today, and forever, and He conquers sin and death, and He brings salvation to His people through His priesthood. And this means: through His priests, through us.

Lord, make us holy men. Lord, make us holy priests, with the virtues that Saint Paul points out to us. He cites, among other virtues, mercy and kindness, patience, forgiveness, and love. Our priesthood has never been more relevant. We have never had so many opportunities in our life to communicate Christ, to serve others by bringing them His mercy and kindness, His patience, forgiveness, and love.

Heralds of Mercy

In the Scriptures there is a strong invitation to forgiveness and pardon: Paul insists on "forgiving one another as the Lord has forgiven you" (Colossians 3:13). And Jesus says, "Forgive and you will be forgiven" (Luke 6:37). Dear brothers, we are recipients of God's pardon; we are ministers of His pardon, and we must therefore always be heralds of His forgiveness, heralds of His mercy.

What wonderful opportunities we have to proclaim the Gospel of mercy and kindness, of peace, justice, and love.

There is a condition, however, and Saint Paul spells it out, saying, "Let the word of Christ dwell in you richly" (Colossians 3:16).

As we recommit ourselves, dear brothers, to the priesthood, let us also recommit ourselves to our lives of prayer in preparation for our ministry of preaching. We are challenged to present the word of God in all its purity, with all its demands, and with all its power.

Often we shall have to say things that will contradict the world on issues of life, and questions of justice, of chastity.

In my homily at an episcopal ordination, I mentioned that a Bishop—and it certainly applies also to all of us as priests—must be a living sign of Jesus Christ. This involves, I explained, being a sign of Christ's compassion and also, with Christ, "a sign of contradiction." Subsequently, a man wrote to me. He could not understand why I used that term. But it is very accurate. It applies to Jesus, to us, and to all priests.

Because we must be living signs of Jesus Christ, we must also be, when necessary, "signs of contradiction."

Dear brothers, we pledge again our lives and our priesthood to reflect the priesthood and person of Jesus Christ in mercy and compassion, in forgiveness and love.

May our Blessed Mother assist us all.

21

Our Vision of Evangelization Transforms Us

Dear brother Priests, dear Friends,

The great reality for which we were called and for which we were ordained is *evangelization,* communicating Christ and His Gospel of salvation—the Gospel of salvation and Gospel of life and peace. The Church constantly offers us this vision as the *inspiration* for all our priestly lives and ministry. This vision of evangelization, which we already possess, and which we must strive to perfect, is truly a transforming reality. It is a *motivating force for our lives and activities,* and it has the power, through the Holy Spirit, to renew us because it explains us to ourselves in such a profound way. My thought is that, if together for a while we can *turn our thoughts* and attention *to the subject of evangelization* and what composes it, we will be consolidating a vision of our ministry that is totally consistent with the Gospel and the life of the whole Church, and totally relevant to what we as priests are trying to be and trying to do.

A few years ago I was visiting a small town in Italy on the island of Sardinia with some members of my office in Rome, and I was struck by a poster that was in the back of a church. And the poster read, "I am not afraid because I love." I subsequently used this slogan in a number of catechetical discussions and found it rather attractive and useful. Eventually, however, I modified it to read, "I am not afraid because I am loved." And then I finally changed it again to, "I am not afraid because I am loved and, therefore, I love."

I believe that these sentiments are very relevant to the sequence of evangelization. When Christ was born, the angel announced to the shepherds not to be afraid. A Savior was born in Bethlehem. In other words, God's love was bringing salvation to the world. Ever since, the Church has been proclaiming the salvific love of God and the need to love in return. "I am not afraid because *I am loved* and, therefore, *I love.*" Or better still, "We are not afraid because we are loved and, therefore, we love."

To Tell the Story of God's Love

When the Holy Father came to the United States in 1987, he mentioned that he had come *to tell again the story of God's love.* And this telling the story of God's love means *the whole proclamation of salvation by word and sacrament.* This proclamation reaches its culmination in the Eucharist—Vatican II has told us this many times—which in turn is the invitation to love God and serve humanity. The story is deeply personal.

In speaking about *the meaning of evangelization*, it is extremely relevant to start with the way Jesus understood Himself in relation to evangelization. In Saint Luke's Gospel he says, "I must proclaim the Good News of the Kingdom of God, because for this purpose I have been sent" (Luke 4:43). These words are a great light for me personally in my service to the Church, and I am sure that they shape my attitude toward the reality of evangelization.

Jesus makes it clear that He is proclaiming His reign or Kingdom, a Kingdom the Church will later on describe as "a Kingdom of truth and life, a Kingdom of holiness and grace, a Kingdom of justice, peace, and love."

As *the kernel and center of the Good News* of His Kingdom, Christ proclaims *salvation*. He insists that He has not come to condemn the world, but to save it. The *Kingdom* and *salvation* are the key words in Jesus' own evangelization. "God so loved the world that he gave His only Son . . . God did not send the Son into the world to condemn the world, but that the world might be saved through Him" (John 3:16–17).

In proclaiming the Kingdom and salvation, Jesus will show how they are related to Himself. He proclaims Himself as *the light of the world* (cf. John 8:12); *the way and the truth and the life* (John 14:6); and again, *the resurrection and the life* (John 11:25–26). In all evangelization what is so important is *the response of faith:* our faith and the faith of our people. When Jesus proclaims Himself before Martha as the resurrection and the life, He insists that whoever believes in Him will never die. He then challenges Martha, *"Do you believe this?"* It is important for Jesus to hear the response. "Yes, Lord" she replied. "I have come to believe that you are *the Messiah, the Son of God."* Jesus is intent on revealing Himself as the Messiah, the Son of God. He does this by *words* and *deeds,* and *signs* and *miracles,* and then by His *death and Resurrection.* And finally, He *infuses His power into a community* that is to be served in a special way by His apostles and *whose deepest identity* becomes *evangelizing* in His name.

22

Near the Cross of Jesus

Dear brother Priests, dear Friends,

It is a joyful privilege for us *to celebrate the gift and mystery of the priesthood.* We celebrate Jesus Christ as He Himself is anointed Priest of the New Covenant and as He shares the priesthood with those whom He has personally chosen. *We express support and love for all the priests* who carry forward their daily dedicated pastoral care of God's people.

All of the dear people of God by their participation show their faith in the Church, in the priesthood, and in the Eucharist. They are all very much aware that, despite the weaknesses and sins of individuals, the Church, which is the Body of Christ, is strong in faith and love. Our hope is in the living God. We believe in the power of the death and Resurrection of our Lord Jesus Christ to forgive sins, to renew hearts, and to bring us all to ever deeper conversion in our lives.

Repentance and Pardon

These times are difficult for all of us and for the people of God. We pray in a special way, with deep fraternal grief and affection, for our brother priests who have been accused, those who, over the years have seriously compromised the priesthood, and those who have been falsely accused. We know that Jesus our High Priest takes on the sins of all of us and offers all of us forgiveness and mercy. As ministers of reconciliation we know how much the world—ourselves included—constantly needs repentance, pardon, penance, and new life. We share the immense pain and suffering of those minors and any others who have suffered through the sins of priests and Bishops. We are called to continually renew our commitment to sacred celibacy and faithful service.

Even as we acknowledge the scandal that has touched our ranks, we are confident in the overpowering grace of Jesus Christ. We feel deep solidarity with tens of thousands of brother priests throughout the United States, and so many more throughout the world, the vast majority of whom are described by our Holy Father Pope John Paul II as those "priests who perform their ministry with honesty and integrity and often with heroic self-sacrifice." He goes on to say: "As the Church shows her concern for the victims and strives to respond in truth and justice to each of these painful situations, all of us— conscious of human weakness, but trusting in the healing power of divine grace—are called to embrace the 'mysterium Crucis' and to commit ourselves more fully to the search for holiness." We are called by God to be part of *a wholehearted reawakening* to those ideals of total self-giving to Christ which are the foundation of our priestly ministry.

The Holy Father continues: "It is precisely our faith in Christ that gives us the strength to look trustingly to the future. We know that the human heart has always been attracted to evil, and that man will be able to radiate peace and love to those around him only if he meets Christ and allows himself to be 'overtaken' by him. As ministers of the Eucharist and of sacramental Reconciliation, we in particular have the task of communicating hope, goodness, and peace to the world" (Address to the Cardinals of the United States, April 23, 2002).

Strong and Committed

It is my conviction, dear brothers, that despite the events that have affected our priestly ministry, you are already part of this search for holiness and this reawakening of the ideals of total self-giving to Christ. And what strength and joy you have in this!

The testimony of our brother priests is simple, sincere, uplifting and exhilarating. One of our brothers expressed these sentiments: "My priesthood is not in crisis. I remain strong and committed to my priesthood. My priesthood is not up for grabs. My priesthood is not an embarrassment. I love my priesthood and, if anything, this gives me the opportunity to live it more fully."

Another brother priest stated, "We find ourselves near the cross of Jesus Christ and that's where the priesthood is the strongest. If we are going to be configured to Jesus Christ, we need to be configured on the cross. As helpless as we may seem, that's where, above all, we are priests."

Another priest shared an experience of encouragement that he had received from a friend who told him: "Jesus is in charge. You are in his care. The Church is safe. You priests are safe. Jesus is risen from the dead. He has conquered all of this. Just submit your priesthood and the Church to Him." He was uplifted by these words, and we are too. Jesus, we trust in you!

Dear brother priests, it is important for all of us to experience as priests *the joy of our ordination*, and to pray in a special way for *vocations to the priesthood*. These vocations are deeply fostered by the witness of your priestly fidelity and joy—*the joy of a special relationship with Christ and therefore with the Father.* We are called to experience the joy of paternity in the Church; to express gratitude for the sentiments of our people, for the love they have for priests. It is the moment to realize the esteem of the faithful for the celibacy that we have promised and that we freely, and with determination, renew today and every day. It is the occasion *to express fraternity among ourselves* in the presbyterate.

It is *because of the priesthood that the Church possesses the Mass,* Viaticum, reservation of the Blessed Sacrament, Eucharistic Adoration, and all the Sacraments. Through the priesthood every vocation is sustained in the Church. *Christian marriage* and *the Christian family* are a special part of the daily pastoral care that priests give to the faithful.

And how grateful we are to the people of God in our parishes for their trust and love and support. We renew our commitment to them because we renew our commitment to Jesus Christ and to the mission of His Church. We are strong not because we have no weaknesses or sins but because Jesus Christ died for us and in the Eucharist His body and blood are offered up to the Father "so that sins may be forgiven."

Dear brother priests, *the people of God count on your love, your pastoral service, and your fidelity to the end.* Jesus Himself has chosen you to serve the rest. You have been anointed to proclaim the Gospel to the poor and to the whole world. Rejoice, be strong, be faithful! You are not alone! Mary, the Mother of Jesus is with you at all times. The prayer of Christ's Church sustains you. And Jesus Himself calls you to sustain, by your love, one another and all your brothers and sisters in the Church.

23

Our Face Set toward Jerusalem

Dear brother Priests, dear Friends,

Let this be a day of praise of God, of *praise and thanksgiving* for the wonderful gift which Jesus Christ Himself bestowed on us: the gift of His Priesthood. It is the gift that He gives to His Church, whereby through the Sacrament of Holy Orders He Himself continues to minister to His holy people, whereby Jesus Christ continues His pastoral activity in the midst of those He loves.

For a few moments, *let us reflect on the word of God* and let us see how relevant it is to ourselves, to all of us.

In the Gospel, Jesus indicates to His disciples that He must go to Jerusalem to suffer, to be put to death, and to be raised up on the third day. This is why Jesus was born. This is why He had come into the world. And now the hour was approaching; it was time to go to Jerusalem! Here we have a very important conversation that reveals so much to us of God's plan of salvation.

Peter comes forward to say no to Jesus: "God forbid, Lord! No such thing shall ever happen to you" (Matthew 16:22). *No*—says Peter—your plan is not acceptable. In effect, Peter is saying, "Jesus, listen to me. What you are doing is not reasonable. As a matter of fact, it is totally absurd. It will not work out. What you are proposing is not correct. *There is another way of doing things: my way!*"

With Immense Joy

But *Jesus knew what He was doing.* He had reflected on this during His entire life—from the time He was young. He knew what His mission was. He had set His face toward Jerusalem and He was going there with immense joy, even though it was going to involve His death. Jesus was going there to offer Himself on the cross, and then to rise again, and finally through His Spirit to communicate power to His disciples. Through His death and resurrection, He would communicate life to the world. Jesus knew that nothing could stop Him.

Peter did not understand. Very often we do not understand, for we try *to judge according to mere human wisdom*—or as it says in the Gospel—"thinking not as God does, but as human beings do" (Matthew 16:23). All the human wisdom in the world cannot equal the wisdom of God. All human calculation cannot figure out the plan of the Paschal Mystery—the death and resurrection of Jesus.

Jesus goes on to tell the apostles that this death and resurrection is not something reserved to Him alone. He says if anyone wants to come after Him, let him "deny himself take up his cross and follow me" (Matthew 16:24). In other words, *the cross belongs not only to Jesus but also to His Church.* And the power of that cross, with the power of the resurrection, belongs to all of us who, as Christians, are called to a sharing in this Paschal Mystery.

Saint Paul tells us, "I urge you by the mercies of God, to offer your bodies as a living sacrifice . . . Do not conform yourself to this age" (Romans 12:1–2). This is where the Paschal Mystery takes us: As followers of Jesus, as His disciples, as members of His Body the Church, we are called upon to have *our share in the cross* and our share in the glory of the cross, our share of the resurrection, which is synonymous with eternal life.

Jesus wills that the mystery of the cross and resurrection should be made sacramentally present throughout the world at every moment of the day. In some place on this earth, *the Sacrifice of Jesus is always being renewed through the priesthood.* The people of God are gathered from the rising of the sun to the going down thereof to offer up the Eucharist in union with Christ and through His priests.

There Is No Stopping

This is what Jesus intended for His priests, and this is what the priesthood is all about. We who are being called to share Christ's pastoral love for His people, express this love in many ways. Day in and day out we are called to be the humble servants of God's people in every circumstance of life. We bring the word of God to His people. We teach, sanctify, and lead. We are to be ministers of reconciliation, examples of prayer, men of compassion, offering help to others at every turn. *But the highest moment in our priesthood is when we offer up the Sacrifice of Jesus.* In the power of the Holy Spirit and surrounded by the people of God, we offer Jesus' death and resurrection to the Father. And through the Eucharist that we celebrate, all the people of God have access through their own active participation to the primary and indispensable source of the true Christian spirit.

During our life, it is our joy always to have a consciousness of the fact that Jesus has chosen us to be servants of His people. Jesus wishes us *to be, above all, the Eucharistic servants of His people*—to offer up His sacrifice whereby He gathers His people into unity. So we are headed now for Jerusalem, and there is no stopping. We are with Jesus and as long as God gives us breath, our role is at His side to offer His sacrifice, to proclaim His death and resurrection sacramentally. In this way, Jesus brings His people to eternal life.

24

So That Sins May Be Forgiven

Dear brother Priests, dear Friends,

The day of your priestly Ordination was *a day of supreme confidence* for you. The Christ who called you and sustained you through many years of preparation ratified His love for you and invited you to be filled with the joy that accompanies His peace.

One of the gifts that Christ gives you is *the word of God* which confirms you in your clear idea of *what the priesthood of Jesus Christ is all about.*

Saint Peter reminds you that Jesus Himself was anointed with the Holy Spirit and power, how He went about doing good and healing all who were in the grip of the devil, and how He commissioned the Apostles to preach to the people and to bear witness to Him.

Dear brothers, like Jesus you were *anointed with the Holy Spirit.* You were sacramentally associated with the ministry of the Apostles and, therefore, commissioned *to preach* to the people, *to bear witness* to Jesus, and *to proclaim the forgiveness of sins.* You were sent out to announce salvation day after day.

Remember always that your priestly role in proclaiming salvation and forgiveness—the salvation and forgiveness brought about by Jesus through His death and resurrection—reaches its culmination as you celebrate *the*

Eucharistic Sacrifice. The Eucharist is central in your priestly life. But even more, it is your greatest service to the people, your greatest contribution to the community.

The reason why you are called to celebrate the Eucharist is expressed in the words of consecration of the wine, ". . . this is the cup of my blood, the blood of the new and everlasting covenant. It will be shed for you and for all so that sins may be forgiven."

Mercy Poured Out

It is through the power of Christ's sacrifice on Calvary, renewed in the Eucharist, that *God's Mercy* is poured out in the world. But it is also through the Sacrament of Penance that *the reconciliation of individual hearts* is brought about. Remember that, like the Apostles on Easter, you were given the gift of the Holy Spirit to forgive sins in the name of the Risen Jesus, who says to you, "Whose sins you forgive, are forgiven them, and whose sins you retain are retained" (John 20:23).

Your ministry, brothers, is *Christ's ministry of mercy.* The mercy of the Eternal Father passes through the heart of the Incarnate Word, and through you heals—as Saint Peter says—all those who are "in the grip of the devil."

In your priesthood there are hundreds of times when you show the love and compassion of the Savior to the poor, the suffering, and those in every type of need. But God never reveals His mercy more through you than when, conscious of your own weaknesses and need for forgiveness, you absolve people from their sins.

Like your brother priests who preceded you, you experience enormous *challenges of service* in the priesthood. But know that God is faithful, God is merciful, above all to those who are His special ministers of mercy. The gift of the Spirit whom you received personally from the Risen Christ confirms you in strength, joy, and peace. He is truly able to remove all fear from your life and give fruitfulness to all your priestly activities.

Faithful to Prayer

Saint Peter does, however, remind you of one more important component in your lives. He says to you, "Remain calm so that you will be able to pray" (cf 1 Peter 4:7). The Second Vatican Council assures you that all your priestly ministry is sanctifying, but it also teaches you that there is a condition for its fruitfulness, namely *union with God through prayer*. My prayer for you, dear brothers, is that you will indeed remain faithful to prayer, and in particular to *the Liturgy of the Hours and prayer before the Blessed Sacrament*. It influences the way you celebrate the Eucharist; it radically affects the content of your homilies; it determines the measure of sensitivity of all your pastoral charity, as well as the degree of your openness to the needs of God's people, and it ensures the authenticity of justice and mercy in your lives.

In prayer, as in so many other aspects of life, Mary the Mother of Jesus is your example and your help. Through her intercession, God provides you strength for service. "That," as Saint Peter says, "in all things God may be glorified through Jesus Christ, to whom belong glory and dominion forever and ever. Amen" (1 Peter 4:11).

25

Marked by Hope and Joy, Suffering and Pain— Always in Love

Dear brother Priests, dear Friends,

The Church rejoices everyday because the mystery of *Christ's call to the Apostles is repeated* and carried on in our midst in your priesthood.

You are associated with the first group of Christ's apostles—the fishermen mentioned in the Gospel. Again and again you hear Jesus speaking to you, saying, "Do not be afraid. From now on you will be catching men."

Yes, *your priestly vocation is to bring the Gospel of salvation to all your brothers and sisters* in the Church and beyond, to help claim the world for Christ, to help the people of our generation to know and love Jesus Christ, the Son of God.

Day after day, the Church gathers with you in prayer. Through the Sacrament of Holy Orders Christ Himself has empowered you to perform your mission. The support of God's people will be with you until the day you die.

But what is this mission of yours, this mission of the priesthood? *What does the priesthood involve?*

It is of course *a sacred service in the Church,* a particular contribution to God's people. In so many ways you are called upon to assist others and to help them contribute to building up the Kingdom of God.

Your own *greatest contribution,* your greatest act of service to the people is *to offer Mass.* The Second Vatican Council told you about this when it said that you fulfill your chief duty in the mystery of the Eucharistic Sacrifice, and that in it the work of our redemption continues to be carried out" (cf. *Presbyterorum Ordinis,* 13).

Your life, like that of your people, is marked by hope and joy, at times by suffering and pain, but always by faith and love.

The Greatest Joy!

Pope John Paul II said that the greatest joy of his life was to share the privilege given to every priest throughout the world: *to be able to celebrate Mass every day.*

You belong to the worldwide group of Catholic priests privileged to celebrate the Eucharist every day, privileged each day, in the words of Vatican II to carry out Christ's work of redemption.

After the Eucharist, what is it that is so important in your life? Saint Paul draws our attention to another great reality of the priesthood when he says, "God . . . reconciled us to himself through Christ and has given us the ministry of reconciliation" (2 Corinthians 5:18). As a priest, you fulfill this ministry of reconciliation in a very specific way: through the *Sacrament of Penance.* In speaking about this Sacrament of Penance, Pope John Paul II has said, "What greater human fulfillment is there than touching human hearts through the power of the Holy Spirit and in the name of the merciful and compassionate Redeemer of the world? Like the laity, our priests must strive to serve in many relevant ways, but they alone can forgive sins in the name of the Lord Jesus. And connected with the forgiveness of sins is new life and hope and joy for the People of God" (*Ad Limina* Address of September 9, 1983).

You Are Not Alone

Your whole priestly life is meant to be *inspired by pastoral love* and modeled on the life of Christ, the one who says, "I am the good shepherd . . . and I will lay down my life for the sheep" (John 10: 14–15).

Obviously, the challenges of the priesthood are many. At times they can seem to be a burden. It is important to realize that *you are not alone.* Christ himself is with you, just as the Father was with Him in His priestly ministry that took Him to the Cross. Remember also that you belong to the sacramental fraternity, which is called the presbyterate. It is important for you *to know and love your brother priests,* to work in close union with them, and to be loved by them. In God's plan for the priesthood, the Bishop represents Christ to you and, in His name, offers you support, friendship, and fraternal love.

There is one more important aspect of your priesthood that I would like to mention at this time: You are to show compassion—to be *a sign of mercy in the Church.* Therefore, your special love is always with the sick and dying; with those in every need; with those in pain and sorrow and suffering of every kind; with those in sin, who have a special need for mercy and redemption.

Finally, remember that at the very moment of your ordination, when the Bishop invoked for you the dignity of the priesthood, he asked God to renew within you *the Spirit of holiness* and to make you a model of right conduct.

The Church entrusted you to the Holy Spirit whom the Church invokes as the Spirit of holiness. As she did so, she reminded you of your *vocation to holiness of life* and of the need for prayer in your sacred ministry. It is an important condition for your supernatural success and for your real joy and personal fulfillment in serving God's people faithfully until the end.

May our Blessed Mother, Mary, the Mother of the Church and the Mother of Priests, be for you today and always *the Cause of your Joy.*

26

A Call to Integrity,
A Call to Holiness

Dear brother Priests, dear Friends,

Recently I was speaking to a Catholic laywoman, a wife, the mother of a family, someone who loves the Church very much. In the conversation she expressed profound esteem for the priests she has known over the years, mentioning how these priests have served the people so well. She likewise spoke of her conviction that through holiness of life priests will find the strength to face all the current problems in the Church. She went on to say that Jesus loves his priests and is faithful to them; she was sure that *their fidelity* to Him will bring many blessings to the Church.

I was very impressed and I tried to remember her exact words, for I knew she spoke the sentiments of millions of Catholics who love the priesthood, their priests, and the Church as Christ founded her. This woman expressed the gratitude of so many people for priests who truly lead holy lives, chaste lives, lives of integrity and priestly dedication.

The Antithesis of Fidelity

The antithesis of all this we have seen in the sad examples of the sexual abuse of children and minors by some of our brothers in the priesthood. Although only a small minority of priests have offended, the scandal has been enormous. Even one case of sexual abuse is intolerable. Children and young people have suffered profoundly, and for this the Church has expressed deep sorrow. Meanwhile, she strives constantly to help victims find healing, peace, and reconciliation. The Church continues to ask victims to come forward to inform both her and civil authorities.

Families have been deeply wounded, and some of them alienated from the community of the Church. Generalizations have hurt the priesthood as a whole, and aspersions have been cast on faithful priests. In the face of all this, there have been false accusations against innocent priests and attempts to punish the community of the Church for the sins and crimes of individuals. The Church herself has been accused of the criminal action of willingly exposing children to grave harm. The gift of priestly celibacy has been ridiculed and the person of the Pope has been denigrated by those who try to implicate him in the responsibility of individual offending priests. Despite mistakes made by some individual Bishops in the handling of offending priests in the past, we know that any charges of criminal conspiracy are absolutely absurd.

Advances in Society and New Responses

The Church is grateful for the advances in society during these recent years toward a fuller understanding of the aberration of sexual abuse of minors, and pedophilia in particular. So many sectors of society are now more attentive to the need to protect children and minors from sexual abuse and to strive to extirpate this abuse from society.

The response to reports of sexual abuse of minors on the part of civil officials, Bishops, parents, and huge sectors of society is different than in the past. The advice that the Church receives today from many psychiatrists, psychologists, and other professionals is different from the advice received some years ago. Throughout all of this, society as a whole has evolved to a greater understanding of this evil.

The Church is convinced that the sexual abuse of the young by anyone is evil because God's law and the human dignity of these persons are violated. Sexual abuse by priests is moreover not only a violation of God's law and human dignity but a violation of the holiness of the priesthood. Any priest who would abuse a young person certainly does not do so acting in the name of the Church. The Church repudiates such actions, because they are essentially contrary to the commandments of God and as such are essentially contrary to the meaning of priestly life and ministry. Pope John Paul II has stated clearly "that there is no place in the priesthood or religious life for those who would harm the young" (Address to the Cardinals of the United States, April 23, 2002).

Universal Need for Integrity and Fidelity

This, dear brother priests, brings us back to our own call to integrity in our life of priestly celibacy. The tragic consequences of the sexual abuse of children and minors show us the great evil caused to victims and their families, to the offending priest himself, to the Church, and to society. The Church insists that this aberration must be eliminated and rooted out not only in the life of any priest, but in the life of every member of society. Even as some efforts have been made to present sexual abuse of children and minors as an evil specific to the Catholic priesthood and the Catholic Church, investigations show that many

areas of society are affected by it in much higher propor-
tions. It continues to plague so many families. Sexual abuse
of the young is repugnant and is to be extirpated in every
individual and in all individuals wherever it is found.

The motivation for Christians and in particular
for priests to avoid this evil is even more pressing than for
others. The holiness of Christianity and the priesthood
also are at stake, as well as the very important question of
human dignity. At the end of the Millennium year celebrations, before the sexual abuse scandal came to light, Pope
John Paul II strongly urged all members of the Church to
pursue the path of conversion of heart and holiness of life.
He insisted that the new Millennium had special exigencies. It required fidelity to the commandments of God and
the Gospel of Jesus Christ. He invited all Christians to
turn to God through Jesus Christ and to be more faithful
to Him than they had ever been before.

We Will Find Strength

Dear brother priests, in our fidelity to God's
commandments, to Christ's Gospel, and to our own priestly
dedication to celibate chastity, we will find strength to serve
all God's people, as the Church has always intended us
to do. We renew our intention to work for the well-being
of all the faithful, young and old. We commit ourselves
anew to protecting children in their innocence and human
dignity, and in bringing them to a full knowledge of Jesus
and His teachings through catechesis and Catholic education. In living upright lives, we will continue to experience
deep joyful fulfillment and find many opportunities to help
build up a civilization of justice, peace, and love.

An essential condition for the effective exercise of our priesthood and the success of all our efforts is fidelity to God's law and the Church's teaching. It is through the Church that our Lord Jesus Christ continually calls us to integrity and to holiness of life.

27

Mercy: The Most Exquisite Form of Love

Dear brother Priests, dear Friends,

You may remember that the Holy Father suggested that, when possible, we choose the Feast of the Sacred Heart of Jesus as our *Day of Prayer for the Sanctification of Priests.*

The Father's Love—The Heart of Jesus

Today and always, our inspiration is the mystery of *the Father's love,* which through the power of the Holy Spirit *passes through the Heart of Jesus* and is signified by His human heart.

We are talking about *the love* of the Father that becomes *tender mercy* in our own life and through our ministry. What then does the mystery of the Father's love revealed in Christ mean for us, for all of us priests? And what does this love mean for our people because of our ministry?

First of all, dear brother priests, you and I have met God's love in our lives under the form of mercy. Deep down we know that *mercy is the most exquisite form of love* for one who has sinned: the most exquisite form of receiving love, the most exquisite form of showing love.

In the Eucharist we receive mercy. Our Holy Father stated the same thing when he visited St. Louis: "In the Mass and in Eucharistic adoration we meet the merciful love of God that passes through the Heart of Jesus Christ" (January 27, 1999). So many Scripture texts speak to us in one way or another about mercy. In the Book of Exodus, the Lord characterizes Himself in these words: "The Lord, the Lord, a merciful and gracious God, slow to anger and rich in kindness and fidelity" (Exodus 34:6). And Moses says, "O Lord . . . pardon our wickedness and sins, and receive us as your own" (Exodus 34:9).

The power of God's word gives us the confidence to continue, in the words of Psalm 25, to invoke the Lord saying: "Remember your mercy, Lord, and the love you have shown from of old" (Psalm 25:6).

God's Love in the Face of Our Sins

What is the Lord telling us? The message is one of *personal love that shows itself as mercy.* What is mercy? It is simply *God's love for each of us in the face of our sins, our weaknesses, our needs.*

What is so important for us is that we pause, amidst many pastoral responsibilities and good works, to reflect on *how much the Father has loved us in Christ* the High Priest, in Christ the Good Shepherd. Not only has the Father forgiven our sins, been merciful, compassionate, and kind to us at every moment of our lives, but He has chosen us in Christ for the ministry of mercy, compassion, and kindness.

My brother priests, over and over again we have received mercy through Christ who assures us of His love, *laying down His life for us.* What a magnificent Gospel passage we have in the tenth chapter of Saint John where

Jesus tells us five times that He lays down His life, gives His life for us. He tells us that He lays down His life freely. He insists on having the *power* to lay down His life.

This reminds us that *we are loved,* that this love is mercy in our lives; it is compassion, pardon, forgiveness. This love received as mercy that passes through the Heart of Christ also means that we are called to dedicate ourselves generously to *our ministry of mercy.* Our response to the mercy revealed by the Good Shepherd laying down His life for us is a commitment to show the Father's mercy, Christ's mercy, through our whole lives as priests, but especially through our ministry of forgiveness and reconciliation.

Reflecting on God's love for us then and rejoicing in it, we have the joy of knowing that we are called, as priests, *to extend mercy, kindness, and compassion.*

The problems of our lives and the challenges of our ministry remain. But, my brother priests, how much it means to us *to be loved by the Father* and the Son, and through the power of the Holy Spirit *joyfully to reveal mercy,* pardon, and kindness to the people of God. The priesthood is truly fulfilling, truly worth living!

28

What Does Jesus Mean to You? What Do You Mean to Jesus?

Dear brother Priests, dear Friends,

What does Jesus mean to you? In the word of God, in the Book of Revelation, we hear Him called "the faithful witness, the firstborn of the dead," the one who "loves us and freed us from our sins by his blood" (Revelation 1:6).

Jesus is indeed *faithful* to His Father and to the mission that His Father gives Him. And in that fidelity He brings glad tidings to the lowly, glad tidings to the poor. Jesus is then the faithful witness who challenges us to proclaim in fidelity and joy His saving Gospel. What does Jesus mean to you? He means *fidelity*. Your fidelity to the priesthood and to the Church is possible because of His fidelity. Your fidelity is absolutely required because of His fidelity.

Jesus is *our great High Priest*, the friend who personally called you to share His Priesthood, and the one who has loved you, and whom you have endeavored to love and follow. What does Jesus mean to you? He is our Shepherd, the type and model of all our pastoral ministry. At the same time He is the example for our generosity, the inspiration for our joy, the strength for our priesthood and for the faithful offering of our lives.

But *what do you mean to Jesus?* As His brother priests you are important to Him. You are important to His plan of salvation, important for His Church. Accept once again these words of the Book of Revelation as having special meaning for yourselves in the midst of God's people. You heard proclaimed that Jesus "loves us and freed us from our sins by his blood," that He has made us "a kingdom of priests for his God and Father" (Revelation 1:6).

My brother priests, *you have been loved* and redeemed by Christ and entrusted with the Eucharist and, therefore, with the mystery of redemption for our brothers and sisters. What love! What trust! What confidence Christ places in you! Christ shares with you the mission given to Him by His Father. His trust in you is at the center of all collaborative ministry. *Christ needs you.* He needs your heart, your hands, your mind—your love. Christ *needs your renewed and absolute fidelity.*

Jesus—Faithful Witness

And all of this implies that Christ needs *your perseverance* amidst the joys and sorrows, the anxieties and trials, the hopes and disappointments of your daily lives as His priests serving God's people. Jesus, the faithful witness, insists on your personal fidelity. He calls you in spite of your imperfections, the limitations of your humanity, your weaknesses and your sins. He is always ready—in His love—to forgive you, to encourage and challenge you.

Are you important for Jesus and His Church? Most assuredly! And is your effort valuable? And is your continued conversion necessary? And is your renewed fidelity to Christ a priority in your priestly lives and in your service to our people? We know that the answer is *yes.*

Proclaim this clearly: *Tell the world that you love Christ and His priesthood* and *you intend to live your vocation faithfully until death. Christ wants the world to know that He loves His priests,* that He stands by you and supports you, and, yes, asks a great deal of your love and generosity.

In dealing with the mystery of the Church, the Second Vatican Council says that the Bishop, by reason of his role, is the Vicar of Christ for his people, just as the Pope is the Vicar of Christ for the universal Church. In the Bishop, joined with his priests, our Lord Jesus Christ is present in the midst of those who believe (cf. *Lumen Gentium,* 21). This is, of course, a formidable responsibility, one that calls Bishops and priests to live in ever greater unity. It also gives the Bishop the responsibility constantly to proclaim Christ's love—love for His people and love for you, His priests.

My brother priests, my desire is to do just that— to proclaim Christ's love for you—and in the name of Jesus our brother and High Priest to thank you for what you *are* and for everything you *do* to bring glad tidings to the poor.

29

Have No Fear!

Dear brother Priests, dear Friends,

After the laying on of hands, during your priestly
ordination, you heard the prayer of the Church with which
the handing on of the priesthood was accomplished:
"Grant, we pray, Almighty Father, to this your servant the
dignity of the priesthood; renew deep within him the Spirit
of holiness. . . ."

It is very impressive that, at the moment when the
Church transmits the power of the priesthood, she asks
the Father to send forth upon you the Holy Spirit. And the
Church identifies this Spirit as *the Spirit of holiness*—the
Spirit who alone can make you holy and enable you, by
the example of your manner of life, to instill right conduct
in others. In the very act of transmitting priestly power,
the Church speaks about the holiness that comes from the
Spirit of God, the holiness that is so necessary if you are to
fulfill your priestly ministry.

But what is your priestly ministry? The word of
God gives us so many insights into *why we priests exist*—
who we are and what we are to do.

We believe that God chooses. We believe that the
prophecy spoken to Jeremiah applies to you: "Before
I formed you in the womb I knew you; before you were born
I dedicated you" (Jeremiah 1:5). And, reflecting further on

the words of the Prophet, we hear God continue to speak:
"To whomever I send you, you shall go; whatever I command
you, you shall speak. Have no fear before them. . . . See,
I place my words in your mouth!" (Jeremiah 1:7–9).

Day In and Day Out

The *proclamation of the word of God* will always be
the eminent priority in your priesthood. You must speak the
word of God in season and out of season, when convenient
and inconvenient, when acceptable or not acceptable. It
will never, however, be your personal message. It will always
be, as God says, "whatever I command you, you shall
speak." It is the work of a lifetime to proclaim joyfully, faithfully, energetically the word of God that has been revealed
and committed to His Church and that is to be guarded
and taught by her.

Even as you proclaim the word of God, day in and
day out, remember that the proclamation of the word of
God reaches its climax in *the sacramental proclamation of the
Eucharist*. Saint Luke describes for us the scene of the Last
Supper. Jesus "took the bread, said the blessing, broke it
and gave it to them, saying, 'This is my Body, which will
be given for you; do this in memory of me.' And likewise
the cup after they had eaten, saying, 'This cup is the
new covenant in my Blood, which will be shed for you'"
(Luke 22:19–20). The words "do this in memory of
me" are central to your existence as priests and to your
ministry as proclaimers of the Gospel of Jesus Christ.

In the sacramental proclamation of the Mass,
you will renew the death and resurrection of the Lord and
you faithfully fulfill His command, "Do this in memory
of me." The Eucharistic celebration will always take place

through the power of the Holy Spirit. And, in order to be a suitable minister of the Eucharistic sacrifice, you need the Holy Spirit—"the Spirit of holiness"—which the Church invokes on you and communicates to you sacramentally.

You fulfill your chief duty in the mystery of the Eucharistic Sacrifice. In it the work of our redemption continues to be carried out. For this reason, you are strongly urged to celebrate Mass every day, for even if the faithful are unable to be present, it is an act of Christ and the Church" (cf. *Presbyterorum Ordinis,* 13).

Your life, dear brothers, is the Eucharist, and your Eucharistic ministry is what the Second Vatican Council calls "an act of Christ and the Church." All the activities of your life will require an immense amount of *pastoral love*— the pastoral love that you show by being willing to lay down your life for the people of God, the type of pastoral love that is needed for celibacy to be authentic and joyful, the pastoral love that Jesus wants you to give to all His people.

But Vatican II still has a word of deep insight for you. It tells you solemnly that your pastoral love flows mainly from the Eucharistic Sacrifice and that this Eucharistic Sacrifice is therefore *the center and root of your whole priestly life* (cf. *ibid.,* 14). Never forget this truth, dear brothers, and do not neglect to put it into practice. The Spirit of holiness is given to you in ordination, but, forever after, this holiness must be exercised and kept alive through the Eucharist.

The Greatest Human Fulfillment

As priests you serve the people of God in so many relevant ways, but after the Eucharist there is nothing more important than *the ministry of reconciliation* as exercised in the Sacrament of Penance. There is no greater human fulfillment than to touch human hearts through the power of the Holy Spirit and in the name of the merciful and compassionate Redeemer. God has willed *to keep alive in the Church the great gift of His mercy* through the Sacrament of Confession, and only the priest can serve the People of God as the minister of forgiveness and pardon.

In speaking to the Bishops of the United States, the Holy Father has encouraged them *to promote the Sacrament of Penance* and he has charged them to encourage their priests to do the same. I am relaying this charge to you today. But the Holy Father has also encouraged the Bishops themselves to utilize the Sacrament of Penance as penitents. The same is true for you, dear brothers.

Our human weakness will always be with us, and we will always need God's forgiveness. God has chosen you to be priests not because you are perfect or sinless. He has chosen you to be priests, so that, conscious of your own human weakness, and renouncing sin, you can bring, through the Sacrament of Reconciliation, forgiveness to others. This forgiveness was won for all of us by Jesus when He shed His Blood in sacrifice "so that sins may be forgiven."

In Weakness and Humanity

And so you see, dear brother priests, how profound is the reflection of the author of the Letter to the Hebrews: "Every high priest is taken from among men and made their representative before God, to offer gifts and sacrifices for sins." The author of the Letter to the Hebrews goes on to spell out God's plan, saying that every high priest "is able to deal patiently with the ignorant and erring, for he himself is beset by weakness and so, for this reason, must

make sin offerings for himself as well as for other people"
(Hebrews 5:1–3). This is no excuse for sinning or for
remaining in sin, but your weakness and humanity are part
of God's plan to reveal His mercy in the Church and in
the world.

Weakness and sin call for repentance, for a purpose
of amendment, and for a strong resolution to integrity
of life. But realizing your own humanity and weakness, you,
as God's word testifies, are "able to deal patiently with the
ignorant and the erring" *(ibid.)* For all those redeemed
by Christ, repentance and ongoing conversion of heart are
absolutely necessary. But the acknowledgment of weakness
and sin brings about two things in our lives: (1) humility,
which makes us praise God's mercy and forgiveness,
and (2) compassion in reaching out to others who are in
need of encouragement, forgiveness, and mercy.

The forgiveness of sins that was brought about
by the Blood of Jesus, poured out in sacrifice and offered
in the Eucharist, is applied to individual hearts in the
Sacrament of Penance. You must, dear brothers, profit from
this Sacrament, use it humbly, and offer it generously to
the people of God.

With Mary, Mother of Priests

There are numerous other aspects to your priestly
life. You are called by the Church to praise God through
the Liturgy of the Hours, through different forms of prayer,
through the reading of the word of God, and through
the oblation of your will made in union with that of Christ.
Remember that your special love must always be with the
sick and dying, with those in pain and sorrow, and with
those in sin.

As you open your heart to "the Spirit of holiness"—
God's Holy Spirit—realize that you are never alone.
The entire Church is with you and the entire Church will
remain with you in the years to come to support you, to
encourage you, and to be supported and served by you.

The Church asks of you fidelity—fidelity in your
personal commitment to Jesus Christ, to His Gospel, and
to His Church. She asks for your fidelity to prayer. She
asks you to love Jesus Christ, His Church, and His Mother
Mary. As the Mother of priests she is with you always in
your efforts to lead lives of integrity—to be truthful, just,
courageous, merciful, and chaste.

This is truly the hour for you *to trust in the power of
the Paschal Mystery,* to trust that all the weaknesses and sins
of the world are not equal to the power of the living Christ,
the one who invited you to a life of holiness and who says
to you today, "Do this in memory of me."

30

Offering Ourselves with Christ to the Father

Dear brother Priests, dear Friends,

The Offering of Mary and Joseph

We have a beautiful feast that gives so much meaning to our priesthood: *the Presentation of the Lord.* Jesus Himself, who is called "the messenger of the covenant," is offered to His Father in the temple of His glory by His Mother Mary and His foster father Joseph. The prophecy of Malachi is fulfilled: ". . . and suddenly there will come to the temple the Lord whom you seek" (Malachi 3:1).

What a spectacular day in the existence of the Temple! God Himself takes possession of His own temple, through His Son. The Temple was never more glorious: No act of liturgy ever equaled what took place on this day. The magnificence of the Temple's dedication by King Solomon was totally eclipsed by the arrival of the Lord of the Temple.

And the Liturgy of Mary's offering Jesus to the Father would never again be excelled until the day of Calvary when Mary would join Jesus in His own complete and consummated oblation to the Father.

But already in the Temple we have the anticipation not only of Mary's final offering of Jesus, but also *the anticipation by Jesus Himself of His final oblation on the Cross.*

Presented to the Father

The Letter to the Hebrews actually reveals to us the sentiments of the divine Person of Jesus when He came into the world: "Behold I come to do your will, O God" (Hebrews 10:9). These were the sentiments of Jesus at His Incarnation, at His Presentation in the Temple, and at His death on Calvary, when He consummated His act of oblation, His act of loving obedience, when he lay down His life freely and definitively in the Sacrifice of the Cross.

The Second Vatican Council assures us that *the Sacrifice of the Cross* renewed in the Sacrifice of the Mass is the source and summit of all Christian life and, at the same time, *what the Catholic priesthood is all about.* It is about Christ's offering of Himself to the Father—an offering that began at the Incarnation, was renewed in the Temple at the Presentation, and was consummated on Calvary.

The Christ, who offered Himself in sacrifice, shares with the Church the role of teaching all of us to offer ourselves in union with Him to the Father. The Church, in turn, counts on the Seminary *to lead our candidates for the priesthood to a greater sharing in Christ's oblation.* It is fitting that the men called by Christ to act in His person and to renew sacramentally His sacrifice should be trained in His sentiments of self-oblation in order to be worthy ministers of His Sacrifice.

The Jesus, who offered Himself totally to the Father, was, in the words of the Letter to the Hebrews, "a merciful and faithful high priest" (Hebrews 2:17). He was also in the words of Simeon meant to be "a sign of contradiction."

The Seminary exists to help our young men be configured to Jesus in His important role as merciful and faithful high priest and sign of contradiction. As priests you are called to keep alive and pass on to the priests of tomorrow these high ideals.

31

Generous Celibate Love

Dear brother Priests, dear Friends,

If we ask one another what *the greatest treasure of our lives is,* we will undoubtedly say that it is the *priesthood.* This priesthood is exercised through generous celibate love. It involves the proclamation of the Gospel, especially its sacramental Eucharistic proclamation; it is a life of prayer and sacrificial service to the people. Priests, in effect, with Jesus, have *laid down their lives for their friends.*

In the Gospel Jesus speaks to us about just this, saying, "No one has greater love than this, to lay down one's life for one's friends" (John 15:13).

The Answer Is Yes!

If we ask the question, Is this life difficult? We would have to admit that, yes, there are difficulties in a life of sacrifice. But then we would have to ask the question, Is this life *joyful, satisfying, fulfilling?* And the answer is *yes!*

Once again Jesus speaks to us in the Gospel, saying, "I have told you this that my joy might be in you and your joy might be complete" (John 15:11). Yes, the priesthood is *a deeply fulfilling life.* The priesthood, after our Baptism, is the greatest honor of our lives. And that is why we are now *focusing on the priesthood and praying for vocations to the priesthood.* We are asking God to give the gift of this *calling* to many young men, because the Church needs more priests, more servants of the Gospel to fulfill the needs of God's people, to lead them to Christ.

The Lord says: "It was not you who chose me, but I who chose you and appointed you to go and bear fruit that will remain" (John 15:16). Every vocation to the priesthood is then *a personal calling from Christ*. It represents a choice that He makes, a gift that He gives. *We are asking the Lord* to continue to choose, to continue to call young men to the priesthood, to continue to give them the generosity to accept the work of the priesthood and the joy and strength to persevere in it.

Always Another Christ

The priesthood of Jesus Christ is so important for the Church. And every man who shares this priesthood is important, important in God's plan, important for God's people, not only for *what* he does, but also for *who* he is: *another Christ*. This applies to the newly ordained, to the Pope himself, to all the active and zealous priests, to those retired and dedicated to prayer and, sometimes, to suffering for the Church. The role of being another Christ is challenged but never obliterated by human weakness. The priest is *constantly called to conversion and renewal*, just like all his brothers and sisters.

We have many witnesses—many zealous and joyful priests—who want to proclaim to everyone that *the priesthood is a wonderful vocation* and that they are very grateful to God for having been called to it personally by Christ. They want everyone to know how fulfilling it is to celebrate the Eucharist, to forgive sins in the name of Jesus, to teach the faith and to stand with the people of God at all moments in their lives: to share their joys and their sorrows, their anxieties and their hopes.

32

The Joy of Building the Civilization of Love

Dear brother Priests, dear Friends,

The whole Church rejoices on the feast of Holy Thursday. We remember the words that the Holy Father spoke in St. Louis in 1999. He said at the end of Mass: "Peace—the peace of Christ to all. . . . A special greeting to the priests, who carry forward with love the daily pastoral care of God's people."

On Holy Thursday *we proclaim Jesus Christ as the great High Priest anointed by the Holy Spirit.* We remember the words He applied to Himself: "The Spirit of the Lord is upon me. . . . he has sent me to bring glad tidings to the lowly" (Isaiah 61:1).

We are privleged *to celebrate the gift and mystery of the priesthood.* We celebrate Jesus Christ as He Himself is anointed Priest of the New Covenant and as He shares the priesthood with those whom He has personally chosen. On Holy Thursday the faith of the Church links the priesthood to the Eucharist and the Eucharist to the priesthood. It is the day on which *we express support and love for all the priests,* who do exactly as the Holy Father says: "carry forward with love the daily pastoral care of God's people."

The Whole Community Is Involved

Holy Thursday is the day to remember *the anointing of Christ and the anointing of our priests.* It is the day when *the Church blesses the holy oils,* especially the Chrism with which priests are anointed, but with which also all Christians are anointed in Baptism and Confirmation and conformed to Christ.

My brother priests, *the people of God support you and encourage you.* The whole community needs the Eucharist; they need your sacramental ministry; they need your priestly service. Their holy Catholic faith embraces belief in your special priestly vocation put at their service by Christ the Priest. The young and old encourage you by their prayers as you renew the promises of your priesthood and restate in freedom—absolute personal freedom—*the commitment you generously made to celibacy* at the time of your ordination.

Experience the Joy

Dear brother priests, Holy Thursday is the day for all of us to experience as priests *the joy of our ordination.* This is the day for the Church to pray in a special way for *vocations to the priesthood.* These vocations are deeply fostered by the witness of your priestly joy. This is the day for all priests to experience *the joy of a special relationship with Christ and therefore with the Father.* We are called to experience the joy of paternity in the Church; to express gratitude for the sentiments of our people, for the love they have for priests. It is the moment to realize the esteem of the faithful for the celibacy that we have promised and that we freely renew. It is the occasion *to express fraternity among ourselves* in the presbyterate.

It is *because of the priesthood that the Church possesses the Mass,* Viaticum, reservation of the Blessed Sacrament, Eucharistic Adoration, and all the Sacraments. Through the priesthood every vocation is sustained in the Church. *Christian marriage and the Christian family* are a special part of the daily pastoral care that priests give to the faithful. In a recent Holy Thursday letter to the priests of the Church, the Holy Father repeated *the esteem for priests* that he expressed in St. Louis. I want you to hear these words:

> I write . . . to you, dear Brothers in the priesthood, with Holy Thursday in mind, picturing you gathered round your Bishops for the Chrism Mass. It is my earnest wish that, as you meet in the communion of your local presbyterates, you may feel united with the whole Church. . . .
>
> In this perspective, how can we fail to give thanks to God as we think of the hosts of priests who, in this vast span of time, have spent their lives in the service of the Gospel, sometimes to the point of the supreme sacrifice of life itself? . . .While confessing the limitations and shortcomings of past Christian genera-tions, and therefore also of the priests of those times, we recognize with joy that a very significant part of the Church's inestimable service to human progress is due to the humble and faithful work of countless ministers of Christ who . . . have been generous builders of the civilization of love.

Dear brother priests, *the people of God count on your love, your pastoral service, and your fidelity to the end.* Jesus Himself has chosen you to serve the rest. You have been anointed to proclaim the Gospel to the poor and to the whole world. Rejoice, be strong! You are not alone! Mary, the Mother of Jesus, is with you at all times. The prayer of Christ's Church sustains you. And Jesus Himself calls you to sustain your brothers and sisters in faith and love.

33

A Shepherd's Care

Dear Bishop-elect, dear Friend,

For a few moments, guided by the Word of God, let us reflect on the meaning of this great mission of yours. First of all, allow me to express the sentiments of gratitude and esteem toward the Bishop who has preceded you and who has served God's people with love, dedication, and generosity of heart. He has labored long and hard to proclaim the Gospel and to serve the Church.

And now *in continuity* with him and his own predecessor, and in the line of apostolic succession you take your place as the new servant pastor of your diocese. As you already know, your episcopal genealogy can be traced through Popes and through many other Bishops in the history of the Church.

Bring Glad Tidings

So much of what your life will be in years to come is explained by a few simple words: "With a Shepherd's Care." But *what is this shepherd's care all about?* Like Peter, you are being asked by Jesus if you love Him. You are repeatedly saying *yes* and He is repeatedly saying to you, as He said to Peter, "Feed my lambs . . . Feed my sheep." (John 21:15, 17)—give my people a shepherd's care. The ministry entrusted to you is the ministry of Christ Himself, High

Priest and Bishop of the Church. It is conferred through
a special outpouring of the Holy Spirit, enabling you, like
Christ Himself, to "bring glad tidings to the lowly and
to heal the brokenhearted" (Isaiah 61:1). By these simple
words of the prophet Isaiah, which Jesus applies to
Himself, you will be guided in your own program of
pastoral service for years to come.

The Second Vatican Council testifies that the
Bishop, assisted by his priests, makes Christ present to the
community of believers. As a diocesan bishop you have
the great dignity of being *a Vicar of Christ* for your people.
It is the same title that the Pope has in relation to the
universal Church. As Christ's Vicar you are called to teach
in His name, to govern by His authority, and to sanctify
by the power of His word and His sacraments. Your
mission is *to proclaim the Gospel of Jesus Christ* day in and
day out. The words of Saint Paul are so very meaningful
for you. Like Saint Paul you can say that in the service
of this Gospel "I was appointed preacher, and apostle and
teacher. On this account I am suffering these things"
(2 Timothy 1:11–12).

Hardships and Hopes

Hardships there will be—you can count on them!—
and *trials* and *anxieties,* together with personal failings.
But not so many as the *joys* and *aspirations,* the *hopes* and
successes of the people of God that will resonate in your
heart—the heart of a Bishop who loves Christ and who, in
response to His command, endeavors to give himself totally,
despite human weakness, for the service of the flock with
a shepherd's care.

Aided by your priests and deacons, you will exercise this ministry in a concrete situation at a determined moment in the history of salvation, within a *community of people* whom you will love intensely. You will give yourself generously to the religious and laity whom the Lord Jesus is now entrusting to your pastoral care. You and your priests will be called to collaborate within a special relationship; your priests will mean everything to you!

What an exhilarating moment, to become Christ's Vicar in a local Church! It is at the beginning of *the third millennium*, which in turn is the greatest anniversary in the history of the world: two thousand years since God became man, since Jesus Christ was born of the Virgin Mary. The whole Church has been mobilizing to be open to the full outpouring of the Holy Spirit, which we have the right to expect in abundance at this special moment in salvation history. And you have the privilege of leading a local Church toward the *conversion of heart* and *interior renewal* that are part of the program of the universal Church.

In Contact with God's People

Everywhere you go you will come into contact with God's holy people, redeemed by the blood of Christ and often making heroic efforts to respond to their Christian vocation. The fervor and zeal of your local Church will be seen in its efforts to be a *community of prayer and worship*, of *justice, truth, and service*. An eminent expression of the authenticity of the Christian life of the diocese is found in its *missionary activity*, its Catholic spirit of solidarity in the faith.

An important dimension of your service will be dedicated to supporting your priests so that they in turn,

with you, can serve the rest of the community with
a shepherd's care. Catholic families are looking for a word
of encouragement in their important mission of communicating love, transmitting life, and teaching the Catholic
faith. So many dedicated single people, young people,
old people, with different gifts and needs will be all around
you, asking you to be their spiritual leader and to show
them Jesus Christ. The poor and the emarginated will have
a special claim to your ministry.

Even as you minister to your own you will surely
be attuned to the great cause of *Christian unity* and
interreligious dialogue and to the important role of civic
collaboration for the good of every citizen of the community.

Meanwhile, in your former diocese and parish you
will be remembered for your faithful service, your support
for your brother priests, your loyal collaboration and,
of course, *your smile* and *kindness.* All these and other gifts
you now bring to your own diocese with the resolve to do
everything out of pastoral love, with a shepherd's care.

To Mirror Christ's Redeeming Love

In speaking to the Bishops of the United States,
Pope John Paul II expressed it this way: "The Bishop is
a sign of the love of Jesus Christ: He expresses to all individuals and groups of whatever tendency, with a universal
charity, the love of the Good Shepherd. His love embraces
sinners with an easiness and naturalness that mirrors the
redeeming love of the Savior. To those in need, in trouble,
and in pain he offers the love of understanding and
consolation. In a special way, the Bishop is the sign of
Christ's love for his priests . . . As a sign of Christ's love
the Bishop is also a sign of Christ's compassion, since he

represents Jesus the High Priest who is able to sympathize with human weakness, the one who is tempted in every way we are and yet never sinned. . . . But the compassion that he signifies and lives in the name of Jesus can never be a pretext for him to equate God's merciful understanding of sin and love for sinners with a denial of the full liberating truth that Jesus proclaimed. Hence there can be no dichotomy between the Bishop as the sign of Christ's compassion and as a sign of Christ's truth."

The Holy Father concluded those remarks by identifying the Bishop as "a *sign of hope* to the people of God, as strong and unbreakable as the *Sign of the Cross,* becoming *a living sign of the Risen Christ.*" You would never think of trying to *do* or *be* any of those things on your own, by human strength. It is Christ who sends you out today in the power of His Holy Spirit.

And so today in the pastoral mission of Jesus Christ a new chapter of grace begins. The continuity of apostolic succession is enacted. The gift of personal renewal is offered to everyone in the community. Everyone is invited to rejoice in hope!

Dear Bishop-elect, the Church entrusts you and your ministry to Mary, the Mother of Jesus, praying that with her help you will always be a sign of hope for the people of God and all your priests. They welcome you. They are ready to embrace you. They are waiting for a shepherd's care!

34

Living Signs of Jesus Christ—
Always with Mary

Dear Bishop-elect, dear Friends,

In a very special way God wills the Bishop to be,
in and through his own humanity, *"a living sign of Jesus
Christ."* Not only does God glorify our humanity but God
uses our humanity to glorify Himself. The Second Vatican
Council and the whole tradition of the Church have spoken
at length on the ministry of the Bishop. In speaking to the
Bishops of the United States our Holy Father has endeavored
to explain so much of the Bishop's identity by stating that
the Bishop is indeed this living sign of Jesus Christ—a sign
that in turn becomes a gift to the Church. The Bishop
stands for Christ and in and through his own humanity
communicates and makes visible Jesus, the Good Shepherd,
to the people of God. The words of Pope John Paul II help
us to understand how far reaching the ministry of the
Bishop is as a living sign of Jesus Christ. The Holy Father
underlines various dimensions of the Bishop as a sign.
This is how he puts it:

- The Bishop is *"the sign of the love of Jesus Christ"*—he
  offers understanding and consolation to those in need.
  In a special way, the Bishop is *"the sign of Christ's love for
  his priests."*

- The Bishop is called to be *a sign of Christ's compassion.*" The Holy Father explains this further, saying, "The consciousness on the part of the Bishop of personal sin, coupled with repentance and with the forgiveness received from the Lord, makes his human expression of compassion ever more authentic and credible. But the compassion that he signifies and lives in the name of Jesus can *never be a pretext* for him to equate God's merciful understanding of sin and love for sinners with a denial of the full liberating truth that Jesus proclaimed. Hence there can be *no dichotomy* between the Bishop *as a sign of Christ's compassion* and *as a sign of Christ's truth.*

- The Bishop is truly then *a sign of fidelity to the doctrine of the Church.*" He is never reticent to proclaim the teaching of the Church, which he embraces with all his heart, together with his brother Bishops and in communion with the Roman Pontiff, in virtue of a charism sustained by the Spirit of Truth.

- Another role assigned to the Bishop is to be *a teacher of prayer,*" and as such he is *a living sign of the praying Christ.*" Like Christ, the Bishop is called to submit all his pastoral initiatives and decisions to the Father. Jesus did nothing without praying.

- The Bishop is called moreover to be *a sign of the unity of the universal Church.*" We are never more ourselves than when we embrace the Church's universal faith and discipline, and are open in charity to the needs of the universal Church. Sometimes we are asked why we give to the Church's missions, why we help those far away, why we offer support to the Pope when there are so many needs at home. The universal Church and our belonging to her prevent us from ever becoming a sect turned in on ourselves and oblivious to the needs of others through-out the world. Yes, the Bishop is indeed called to be *"a sign of Catholic solidarity."*

- As a living sign of Jesus Christ, the Bishop cannot renounce the preaching of the Cross. Like Jesus, he must accept criticism and acknowledge failure in not being always able to obtain a consensus of doctrine acceptable to everyone. Because he is *"a sign of fidelity,"* he must therefore also be *"a sign of contradiction."* Jesus was a sign of contradiction. Despite necessary openness and gentle dialogue, the Bishop, too, must be the same sign of contradiction in the world.

- Finally though, in the words of the Holy Father, the Bishop is meant to be "*a sign of hope* for the people of God, as strong and unbreakable as *the sign of the Cross,* becoming *a living sign of the Risen Christ.*"

As a priest, you have striven to be a living sign of Jesus Christ in the deep fulfillment of your priesthood. From now on you are meant to bear joyful witness as a Bishop. Everything you do, beginning with the proclamation of the word of God that culminates in its Eucharistic celebration, you must do in the contagious joy of your episcopal ministry.

Among the many tasks that will be yours, you are asked to give very special attention to coordinating all the efforts of the local Church in promoting vocations to the priesthood because every vocation in the community of the Church needs the Eucharist and, therefore, the priesthood. You will always exist for the community, the Eucharist, and the priesthood!

In this work and in everything else you do as a living sign of Jesus Christ, you will be supported by the people of God, by your brother priests, and your brother Bishops in the Episcopal Conference. You will continue to be confirmed in your faith by the Successor of Peter. Always with Mary you will be sustained by God's grace through her intercession. In her glorious Assumption she is herself "a sure sign of hope" for us all.

35

Strong and Unbreakable
as the Sign of the Cross

Dear Bishop-elect, dear Friends,

The Spirit of God, acting through the ministry of Peter the Apostle, *has designated you a Bishop in the Church of God.* With Saint Paul you are now ready to say, "In the service of this gospel I have been appointed preacher and apostle and teacher, and for its sake I undergo present hardships" (2 Timothy 1:11–12).

Not only has the Spirit of God indicated His eternal election of you for the office of Bishop, but the Church herself transmits to you the sacred powers of a servant leader. She is here to proclaim that you are today and forever the servant of the Gospel for the hope of the world.

The Church is here! The Church is with you! *Our Holy Father is present* in our midst through his Representative, and with the presence of the Holy Father is the guarantee of your union in and with the universal Church. You are inserted into the worldwide College of Bishops, with a responsibility to all your brother Bishops and to all the faithful of the Catholic Church. For you have truly been appointed "preacher and apostle and teacher" of the Catholic faith.

The Church Is with You!

The Church is with you! According to the ancient practice of the Church, dioceses are gathered together in provinces in order to pursue the pastoral good of God's people. As Bishop you will be linked with the province and *your Metropolitan Archbishop.* In the years to come he will be your first support in the College of Bishops. You must be convinced from this day on that you will never be left alone to shoulder the burdens of the Episcopacy. In the fraternity of your Metropolitan Archbishop and so many other Bishops you will find the strength spoken of by Saint Paul— "the strength that comes from God"—to bear "your share of the hardship for the Gospel" (2 Timothy 1:8).

The Church is with you! Your own beloved Church, your priests and deacons, your seminarians, your religious, your laity, all ready to follow your servant leadership in continuity in the life of this local Church represented by your predecessor. He himself offers you the Church that he endeavored to serve faithfully and assures you with simplicity and deep sincerity that he wishes to be of service to you in any way possible. You will meet thousands of your flock who will gather with you in the Eucharist that you will celebrate throughout the Diocese. What a privilege it is for you to lead this Church in the New Millennium of grace and mercy, relying on the help of our Lord Jesus Christ, the Shepherd of all Shepherds, the Head of the Church.

The Church is with you! So many people who have loved you for years are with you. These include your priest friends, your seminarians, so many people who have benefited from your ministry over the years. It could not be otherwise. The Church of your Baptism, the Church of your priestly ministry joins with you in exultation and prayer, promising not to forget you, promising to support you in the years ahead. And how special a grace it is to have your family, your beloved parents, who transmitted to you the faith that you proclaim as a Bishop of the Catholic Church.

The entire Church throughout the world looks forward to your testimony, in union with Pope John Paul II and his successors, as a "preacher and apostle and teacher."

A Sign of Christ's Grace and Mercy

In the words of Pope John Paul II, you are meant, as a Bishop, to be *"a living sign of Jesus Christ."* As a living sign of Jesus Christ, you are meant to be *a sign of the love of Jesus Christ,* a sign of the love of the Good Shepherd toward all the people of the diocese. You are called to embrace everyone: sinners, with an easiness and naturalness that mirrors the redeeming love of the Savior; to those in need, in trouble, and in pain you must offer the love of understanding and consolation. As a sign of Christ's love, your special affection is also with the poor, those suffering from injustice, the sick and the dying, and all those striving for holiness of life.

As a sign of Christ's love you are *a sign of Christ's grace and mercy,* for you are able to sympathize with human weakness, as did Jesus who was tempted in every way we are, and yet never sinned.

A Sign of Hope for the People of God

There are many other aspects of your ministry that flow from your call to be a living sign of Jesus Christ, a living sign of His love. Yours is *a ministry of pastoral charity and prophetic leadership.* You are a sign of fidelity to the teaching of the Church, a sign for your people of the certainty of faith. You are a teacher of prayer, the chief liturgist of the diocese. The unity of the Catholic Church is your specialty, even as you reach out in ecumenical and interreligious charity and dialogue. In all of this, however, you are *a servant of the Gospel for the hope of the world.* In Christ, you are *a sign of hope for the people of God, as strong and unbreakable as the sign of the Cross.*

There is one more dimension that the people of God are attentive to with all their hearts. *They know that you love them, but they know that you love them because you love Christ.* They love to hear your dialogue with Jesus; they love to hear you say with Peter in the Gospel, "Lord, you know everything. You know that I love you." But they also love to hear Jesus' response to Peter, His response to you: "Feed my sheep" (John 21:17).

This is where love brings you, where your love for Jesus places you, in the midst of your people, as a servant of the Gospel for the hope of the world.

A Source of Immense Joy

There will always be many aspects in your ministry that will be difficult. Once again, Saint Paul's exhortation— "bear your share of the hardship which the Gospel entails"—reflects deep realism in the life of a Bishop. *Your pastoral love for your people is a source of immense joy in your life and ministry.* Your brother Bishops, your Religious, and your deacons have a special claim on your love, but your priests and seminarians in particular, need your love above all.

With the intuition of their faith, your people have captured the meaning of your ordination. They are asking *that the dialogue of your love for Christ be prolonged.* They are asking you to lead them in proclaiming their own love for Christ and in serving all those who share humanity with Him. For all those whom you are called to serve you are, through God's grace and mercy, a living sign of Jesus Christ, a living sign of Christ's love.

And finally, remember *the Church is with you because Mary, the Mother of Jesus and Mother of His Church, is with you.* She is here with her prayer, interceding for you to be always a living sign of her Son Jesus Christ, a living sign of His love.

36

In the Company of Mary

Dear Bishop-elect, dear Friend,

The Gospel presents to us Mary as she freely and generously consented to be the Mother of the Son of God. In every generation since then Mary has shown her maternal love to all those who are brothers and sisters of her Son, Jesus.

Your Merciful Mother

When Mary appeared in Mexico to the humble Indian Juan Diego—now Saint Juan Diego—her message was an uplifting message of love and hope. She said, "I am your merciful Mother, your Mother and the Mother of all those who live united in this land, the Mother of all those people who love me, who speak to me, who seek me, and who have confidence in me. . . . Am I not here, I who am your Mother? Are you not under my protection? Am I not the source of your joy? Are you not under my mantle. . . ? Do you need anything more?"

Although Mary herself was never a part of the priesthood or the episcopacy, she is *the woman who made all hierarchy possible* because she conceived and bore Jesus Christ our great High Priest, the Shepherd and Bishop of our souls. She is the one whom we recognize in the Gospel as being associated with the Apostles, and whom the Church honors as Queen of the Apostles.

How fitting it is for the Church, on Mary's feast day and under her patronage, to transmit the ministry of the Apostles, to ordain a new Bishop.

We know that every Bishop's ministry involves *responsibility for the Church* beyond the local diocese, including all the missionary activity of the Church. In the exercise of this responsibility we acknowledge the Bishop's special need for *communion with the Successor of Peter*, whose spiritual presence we experience. Episcopal ordination is performed by the mandate and authority of our Holy Father, to whom we express our gratitude and renew our unity in Christ and in the Church.

Before ordination, the Bishop-elect makes a Profession of Catholic Faith and takes an Oath of Fidelity to the Church. One of the things that he swears to do is *to show special love in his ministry to the priests and deacons* who are his collaborators, as well as *to the Religious* of the Church.

He also swears *to promote the dignity of the laity and their particular role in the mission of the Church.*

The ordination of a Bishop is a time to extol all the different vocations in the Church, all the categories of God's people to whom the Bishop ministers, but *especially the priesthood and the family* from which the Bishop comes.

Proclaiming Jesus Christ

This brings us to *the heart of the episcopacy*. We remember how clearly the Second Vatican Council prescribes that the Bishop is to proclaim the faith of the Church. The Council declares that *the proclamation of the Gospel* occupies an eminent place among the principal duties of a Bishop (cf. *Christus Dominus,* 12). It is always understood that the priests are intimately associated with the Bishop in this proclamation, and that *this proclamation reaches its culmination in the Eucharist,* which is the sacramental proclamation of God's word.

We heard Saint Paul's own challenging commitment: "For we do not preach ourselves but Jesus Christ as Lord, and ourselves as your slaves for the sake of Jesus" (2 Corinthians 6:5). As a priest you endeavored to fulfill this role. As a Bishop you must strive to do it with an even greater commitment.

On the part of Jesus, the most effective proclamation of His life was His sacrifice on Calvary when He lay down His life for us. The Bishop is called to lay down his life for the people of God. As he celebrates the Eucharist, which is the renewal of Christ's sacrifice, he is asked to lay down his life for the community.

Your offering, in union with that of Jesus, will guarantee the effectiveness of your proclamation of Jesus Christ as Lord. It will enable you to be, in the words of Saint Paul, "a slave" for the people of God, for the sake of Jesus. It will also express itself in the many other forms of servant leadership that will be asked of you by the Church and by the needs of God's people.

The characteristics of your pastoral ministry are those that marked the ministry of Jesus the Good Shepherd: generosity, compassion, understanding, forgiveness, mercy.

In fulfilling your ministry, you are to be supremely conscious of *the need to trust in Jesus* and in the power of His Paschal Mystery. Whatever the problems, whatever the challenges presented to the Church, you must proclaim that

Jesus Christ is Lord, that He is the Savior of the world, the Lamb of God who takes away the sins of the world, the one Mediator who uplifts God's people and leads us all, through the suffering of the Cross, to the joy of the Resurrection and eternal life in the company of Mary.

37

Servants of Truth and Teachers of Faith

Dear brother Bishops, dear Friends,

In the Gospels we find that Jesus is extremely conscious of being loved by His Father, whom He loves in return and who is always close to Him. Jesus says, "I am not alone." He is conscious of the Father's presence. The Father and Jesus act together (cf. John 8:16).

The Gospels speak about the identity of Jesus as the Son of God. The Successors of the Apostle Peter have kept alive his testimony: "You are the Christ, the Son of the living God."

On the twenty-fifth anniversary of his pontificate, Pope John Paul II recalled the many times he has proclaimed these words, the many times he has renewed, before the world, the faith of Peter, the faith of his successors in the divinity of Christ, which is our holy Catholic faith.

In the Gospel, we hear proclaimed that Jesus perceives a growing hostility to Himself and a lack of understanding of who He is. In this situation He wants His disciples to take a stand on His identity. And so He says, "Who do people say that the Son of Man is?" They replied: "Some say John the Baptist, others Elijah, still others

Jeremiah or one of the prophets." He then said to them, "But who do you say that I am?" And at this point came the reply of Simon Peter: "You are the Christ, the Son of the living God" (Matthew 16:13–16).

Confessing the Identity of Jesus

For all these centuries the Church has meditated on these words, clarifying both the divinity and humanity of Jesus Christ. With Saint Leo the Great we have learned to say that Jesus is "consubstantial with His Father and consubstantial with His Mother." In other words, He is *divine like His Father and human like His Mother* and like us. The Church summarizes this in her beautiful prayer: "Blessed be Jesus Christ, true God and true Man."

Saint Matthew joins to the Confession of Saint Peter the promise of Jesus to found His Church on Peter. The Messiah, whom Peter acknowledges and also confesses as the Son of God, cannot be understood without His people. And so Jesus promises to found His Church—the people of the New Covenant—on the one who, through the power of the Father, acknowledges and confesses His identity. Saint Matthew gives us these wonderful words of Jesus: "And so I say to you, you are Peter, and upon this rock I will build my Church, and the gates of the netherworld shall not prevail against it. I will give you the keys of the kingdom of heaven. Whatever you bind on earth shall be bound in heaven; and whatever you loose on earth shall be loosed in heaven" (Matthew 16:18–19).

All of this signifies that great power was given to Peter. I remember many years ago hearing Pope Paul VI comment on this text. He explained that Peter and his successors were given special powers to serve the community of the Church, but for each one it was to last *only for a season.* Jesus reserved to Himself the ultimate power over the Church. Pope Paul VI explained beautifully how Jesus considered the Church to be forever *His.* In repeating the words of Jesus, Paul VI emphasized one word: "You are Peter, and upon this rock I will build *my* Church" (Matthew 16:18). All of us have the privilege of serving the Church and her mission of evangelization. We know that there is an urgency in our efforts, efforts which the Lord accepts and utilizes, but they are *only for a season.*

The Lord Jesus governs His Church, season after season, through the successors of Peter together with the other apostles. Pope Leo has told us that just as what Peter believed about Jesus is always true, so what Jesus gave to Peter will always endure.

If we read on in the sixteenth chapter of Saint Matthew's Gospel, we see that Jesus is not only the anointed Messiah, who is the Son of God, but He is also the Suffering Servant of the Lord, who indeed requires us to accept Him as our crucified and risen Savior. We must belong to Him in the Church built upon the rock of Peter, who has received from Christ a mission and the power to fulfill it. With Peter we must likewise repent of any past infidelity.

Together We Find Support

We are together, as servants of truth and teachers of the faith, in communion with the Successor of Peter.

It is a blessing for the Bishops to be together. Together we find support because our unity corresponds to Christ's plan to form His Apostles into a group known as the Apostolic College.

It is wonderful for the Bishops to be together with their priests, through whom they are assisted to fulfill their ministry. The Second Vatican Council reminds the Church that it is through the Bishops, together with their priests, that the Lord Jesus Christ is present in the midst of His people (cf. 21).

But it is also wonderful for the Bishops to be together in prayer and worship with members of the people of God—religious and laity.

It is wonderful to assemble with Jesus as His Church. We are the diverse members of His Body. We honor the plan of the Eternal Father for the structure of His Church, built upon Peter and the other Apostles, perpetuated through the ministry of the Pope and the Bishops in communion with him, and sustained by the people of God.

As a community of faith and prayer, a community of love and service, we face together the many challenges present in the Church and in the world. We gather to pray for and commit ourselves, for example, to the great need of forming and supporting holy families, and of perpetuating the priesthood and promoting vocations to it. We gather together to recommit ourselves to the defense, support, and protection of human dignity and human life at every stage, from conception to natural death.

Call to Holiness

Even as we serve others, we are conscious of the Holy Father's call to us as Bishops—his call to holiness in our lives and ministry. Here, too, we count on the prayerful support of the people of God. For even as we pray and strive for holiness, we know that we cannot wait to attain full holiness before encouraging others to do so. And in this way we move forward with humility and resolution, asking once again for the generous and persevering help of the people of God.

In his Post-Synodal Apostolic Exhortation, signed on the twenty-fifth anniversary of his election, Pope John Paul II reflected on this theme: *The Bishop, Servant of the Gospel of Jesus Christ for the Hope of the World.* In this Exhortation, he pointed out both the duty and the needs of the Bishops of the Church, appealing both to them and to the people of God. He said: "The duty of Bishops at the beginning of a new millennium is thus clearly marked out. It is the same duty as ever: to proclaim the Gospel of Christ, the salvation of the world. But it is a duty which has a new urgency and which calls for cooperation and commitment on the part of the whole People of God. The Bishop needs to be able to count on the members of his diocesan presbyterate and on his deacons, the ministers of the Blood of Christ and of charity; he needs to be able to count on his consecrated sisters and brothers, called to be for the Church and the world eloquent witnesses of the primacy of God in the Christian life and the power of his love amid the frailty of the human condition; and he needs to be able to count on the lay faithful, whose greater scope for the apostolate represents for their pastors a source of particular support and a reason for special comfort."

Sent To Be Teacher, Priest, and Pastor

"At the conclusion of these reflections, we appreciate how the theme of the Tenth Ordinary General Assembly of the Synod of Bishops leads each of us Bishops back to all our brothers and sisters in the Church and to all the men and women of the world. Christ sends us to them, even as

he once sent the Apostles (cf. Matthew 28:19–20). We
need to become, for each and every person, in an
outstanding and visible way, a living sign of Jesus Christ,
Teacher, Priest and Pastor."

In doing this, the Bishop will constantly—with
Peter, Leo, and John Paul II—proclaim Jesus Christ as the
Son of the living God and the Suffering and Victorious
Servant of the Lord. And as he does so, the Bishop will
realize that, like Jesus, he is not alone. The Father is with
him. And in the power of the Holy Spirit the people
of God are one with him as he is one with them and with
the College of Bishops and its Head, John Paul II whom
Christ has called to be His servant Vicar on earth.

38

The Bishop and the Promotion of Vocations

(Address to Newly Ordained Bishops, Part I
Rome, July 6, 2001)

Dear brother Bishops, dear Friends,

It is a joy for me to speak with you during this meeting of new Bishops on a topic of great importance for the Church. The theme that I have been assigned actually is a double one and I shall treat it as such. It is, *The Bishop and the Promotion of Vocations.* And, secondly, *The Pastoral Care of Seminaries.*

This theme is of great relevance both to the diocesan Bishop and to auxiliary Bishops, because it so deeply concerns the life of the Church.

In the Context of Vatican II

In our address today, in speaking about vocations, it is understood that we presume the whole teaching of the Church as a background and context. The Bishop is the father and shepherd of the whole community. As a consequence, in his ministry *the Bishop is called upon to promote and coordinate all charisms* in the Church. He extols the nature of the Body of Christ and gives everyone a sense

of dignity, great worth, and importance. The Bishop is
constantly aware of what Saint Paul says, "There are different kinds of spiritual gifts but the same Spirit; there are
different forms of service but the same Lord; there are
different workings but the same God who produces all of
them in everyone" (1 Corinthians 12:4–6).

The Bishop is the Church's witness to the teaching
of the Second Vatican Council on *the Church as the people
of God.*

Whether the Bishop is a member of an institute
of consecrated life or not, he extols for the people of God
the value of consecrated life. He teaches how much consecrated life means for the Body of Christ. He supports
religious in their consecration and mission. He is a friend
of religious and constantly lets them know how much
the Body of Christ needs them.

The Bishop is the faithful proclaimer of *the doctrine
of Vatican II on the laity.* He speaks frequently of the universal
call to holiness. He spends a great deal of time explaining
to the faithful the relevance of *Lumen Gentium* and *Apostolicam
Actuositatem* for the laity. In this regard, let us recall for just
a moment a famous discourse of Pope Pius XII. He gave
it in 1946 on the occasion of the creation of new cardinals.
My predecessor, Cardinal Glennon of St. Louis, was among
them. The famous phrase at the time was Pius XII's
assertion "The laity are the Church." Obviously, he did not
mean this in any exclusive sense. Obviously, the laity are
no more the Church than are the religious, the deacons, the
priests, the Bishops. What Pius XII endeavored to communicate was that the laity, however, *are* the Church; that
they are not some appendage to the Church. It is not that
they *only belong* to the Church; it is not that they *only work*
in and for the Church; it is the fact that they *belong to the*

essence of the Church—*they are the Church.* This teaching of
Pius XII is so beautifully summarized in Vatican II. When
we study the fonts of Vatican II we realize that the most
frequently cited individual source of Vatican II is Pope Pius
XII and, hence, his teaching on the laity is so much a part
of the legacy of Vatican II, so much a part of what is
presumed when we as Bishops speak about vocations in the
Church. The role of the laity is of supreme importance. But
today we are emphasizing another role—that of the priest.
We are doing this in an ecclesial context and in no way do
we slight the dignity and mission of the laity.

In yet another sphere—in those places where the
permanent diaconate functions—the Bishop finds himself
as the great promoter of the permanent diaconate and
considers himself fortunate to have as his collaborators in
Sacred Orders permanent deacons. The Bishop extols this
ministry and invites men to consider it in those countries
where the episcopal conference has established it. This
is certainly the case in the United States of America. The
Bishop promotes this vocation and guides it by establishing a program of demanding formation for all these
men who will be ordained. He also integrates the permanent deacons, as well as their wives, into the apostolate
of the diocese. The permanent diaconate is then an important category in the Church, but this is not what we are
speaking about today.

Holiness Is Attainable

The Bishop constantly appeals to every category
of the people of God to accept the challenge of discipleship, to commit themselves to the new evangelization and
to all the needs of the local Church and beyond, and to

realize that *holiness* is attainable in that vocation to which divine providence has led each person.

The Holy Father is a great leader of the Church in proclaiming the universal call to holiness. He does this in a special way by his particular solicitude in beatifying and canonizing members of the Church. How comforting to know that in the twentieth century two hundred and seventy laypersons were beatified, and two hundred and fifty laypersons were canonized, so many of them by Pope John Paul II. What is evident is that every person is called to exercise specific gifts, and this enriches the Body of Christ. In the community of the baptized *holiness is the goal of all.*

This attitude of loving support on the part of the Second Vatican Council for all the categories of the Church is presumed in our discussion on today's theme: *The Bishop and the Promotion of Vocations.* Here, however, we have no hesitancy in concentrating on one particular area of vocations in the Church: *the vocation to the priesthood of our Lord Jesus Christ.* It is an area of supreme importance to the local Church and to the universal Church. Vocations to the priesthood facilitate Christian living at every level. No priesthood, no Eucharist! No Eucharist, no Church!

The Bishop's Faith and Joyful Trust

The promotion of vocations to the priesthood is, therefore, *the work of the entire community.* It is required for the good of the community. But the leader of the community, the one who must be the first to perform this activity and exercise this responsibility is *the Bishop.* In the opening paragraphs of its decree on priestly formation *Optatam Totius,* the Second Vatican Council highlights the Bishop's coordinating role in promoting vocations, as well as the active partnership with him to which all the people of God are called.

Let us, therefore, look at this responsibility and reflect on the activities by which it is fulfilled. Obviously, the ordinary of a diocese shares first of all with his auxiliary Bishop this great responsibility and mission.

Essential in fulfilling this responsibility and a prerequisite for every activity of the Bishop in this field is *his attitude of faith and trust.* The Bishop must believe in *the power of Christ's Paschal Mystery.* The Bishop must believe that the Crucified and Risen Christ has the power today, even in the midst of all the extraordinary challenges that young men face, to attract them to Himself and to His celibate priesthood. Every activity of the Bishop as a promoter of vocations expresses this faith, and applies this faith in an attitude of joyful trust.

The faith of the Bishop in the power of Christ's Paschal Mystery, together with the manifestation of this faith in joyful trust, is a great gift to the local Church. The local Church needs to be constantly uplifted by the faith and joyful trust of the Bishop. At the core of all vocation promotion is the question that Jesus Christ puts to His Church, but first to His Bishops: "Do you believe this?"—*Credis hoc?*—(John 11:26), and in another context, "Do you believe that I can do this?" (Matthew 9:28). And the answer that the Bishop must give is, Lord Jesus I believe in the power of your Paschal Mystery. Jesus, I trust in you! And, if we believe, we must proclaim this belief. Our people must experience our faith and witness our joyful trust. The grace of the Sacrament of Holy Orders has not been given to us in vain.

I am convinced, dear brothers, that our faith and trust are linked together. The one who demonstrates such faith and challenges us to trust is our Holy Father John Paul II.

A Single Lesson of Hope

Permit me to share with you two aspects of single experience—or at least a single lesson of hope.

Many years ago I had the opportunity to visit Ukraine. It was 1963, during the height of the Communist persecution. The ecclesial community was oppressed. I am convinced that it was very difficult for people to trust in God's providence. I am sure, however, that many people did.

I recall visiting a Latin rite Church in the city of Lviv, the only such Church open for worship. I spoke to the old priest as best I could in Latin. I asked him if I could offer Mass. He told me that he could say Mass but it would be dangerous for him to let me say Mass in his Church. There was a man in the rear of the Church and the priest told me he was a government spy. I asked him if there were any seminarians to be ordained. He replied that *the priestly ministry would terminate with him*—at least that is what I understood.

We all know the extraordinary faith and trust of our Holy Father and his determination to challenge the Church to have faith and trust in the power of Christ's Paschal Mystery. In this faith and trust John Paul II has entered into paschal conflict with all the powers of darkness, encouraging the Church not to be afraid. He has constantly held out hope for Eastern Europe.

Thirty-eight years later I was once again in the city of Lviv, this time in the company of John Paul II. One million three hundred thousand people, perhaps one million five hundred thousand, participated in the Holy Father's Mass. Young seminarians, of both the Ukrainian and Latin rite were everywhere to be seen. Two seminaries have been built with the help of other local Churches. The Catholic Church has emerged from persecution and near extinction. John Paul II has never wavered. He is convinced that the perennial power of *the Paschal Mystery is unleashed in prayer, patient work, and trust.* This is the example he sets for the Church and for us Bishops in particular.

It seems to me that John Paul II has repeatedly responded to Christ's question: Do you believe that I can do this?

Personal and Energetic Involvement of the Bishop

In the Bishop's role of promoting vocations I believe it is important to emphasize that the Bishop must be *personally and energetically involved* in the recruitment of vocations. If, generically, a Bishop is the diocesan vocation director who summons all the faithful to respond to the universal call to holiness and to their specific vocation— and he is—he is also the *chief diocesan vocation director for candidates to the priesthood.* This role cannot be relegated to a diocesan official or a diocesan office. However, the appointment, where possible, of a particularly happy, faithful, articulate, and enthusiastic priest to be the Bishop's delegate in serving as the diocesan director of vocations to the priesthood is of high priority.

The Bishop needs *personal contact with prospective candidates* for the priesthood. The Bishop must constantly extend personal invitations to candidates whom he meets: young boys, young men. The Bishop must be known as

one who brings up the subject and speaks about it
constantly. In this regard he must also be willing to meet
with candidates personally, one on one. I myself have found
it useful to preach a weekend retreat to a group of young
men who accept my invitation. It is called *a discernment
retreat*. Through my diocesan vocation office, I have been
given the names of young men who are interested in a
vocation. The vocation office, in turn, receives a large
portion of these names from pastors or from other priests
who have had contact with these young men, whose names
are then passed on to me. One year I had the names of
one hundred young men. I invited all of them to a weekend
retreat. Twenty-three of these young men accepted my
invitation. It was a very uplifting event and proved to be an
opportunity for grace. It began on a Friday afternoon. We
held it at the Seminary. On Saturday and Sunday the young
men assembled for the celebration of the Eucharist.
I celebrated for them on Saturday. I also was able to speak
to them on four occasions; I gave them four separate
conferences. I met each one individually for a quarter of an
hour. Of the twenty-three retreatants, fifteen pursued the
enrollment in the seminary. Eleven were accepted. All
the young men told me that it was very important for them
to see *the personal interest of the Bishop in their lives*. The
value of personally being invited to consider a vocation to
the priesthood cannot be overestimated.

One of the important activities of the Bishop is
to continue to gather the names of young men who will listen
to an invitation to the priesthood, young men who are
willing to discuss the possibility. Hence, the Bishop should
confer with high school chaplains, university chaplains, and
parish priests to make sure that candidates know that he
is willing to meet personally with them. Obviously, he does

not assume the more extended role of the director of
vocations in the diocese, but his personal interest means
a lot to an inquiring young man. What is also at stake
is *the personalism of the Church*, the personal interest of the
Good Shepherd.

On various occasions, when there are assemblies of
young people in a diocese, it is so opportune to speak about
vocations to the priesthood. This happens in my
Archdiocese on the occasion of *the Chrism Mass* on Holy
Thursday. We have a large cathedral, and besides inviting
the priests we also invite hundreds of children from
Catholic schools. The topic of vocations to the priesthood
is easily linked to a reflection on the readings for Holy
Thursday. This presentation is always made with full
respect and understanding of the vocation of every young
person; yet we must have no reticence in speaking explicitly
about vocations to the priesthood.

Each Bishop can determine what is possible in his
situation, how contacts with young people can be made
and how extended they can be. Another successful endeavor
is for a Bishop *to offer a dinner* for young men who are
brought to him by a vocation director. Telling *the story of his
own vocation* is certainly interesting for these young men
to hear. Being given the opportunity to speak to the Bishop
in the presence of one or two young priests is also an
excellent means of promoting vocations.

One of the most effective moments of the Bishop's
pastoral ministry is the assembly in which young people
receive *the Sacrament of Confirmation*. In a single year I am
able to go to so many parishes in the Archdiocese and meet
thousands of young people. There are also Confirmation
ceremonies in the cathedral where different parishes
assemble. In all of this there are so many opportunities for

me and my auxiliary Bishops to have contact with young men and constantly to invite them to consider, under the action of the Holy Spirit, the possibility of a vocation to the priesthood.

Creating an Atmosphere in the Diocese

Another role of the Bishop is to create in the diocese *an atmosphere that encourages vocations.* There are some leadership gurus, some very successful leaders in the world, who tell us that an effective leader has only three or four clear goals from which he will not be distracted. Every Bishop, whether a diocesan ordinary or an auxiliary Bishop, must have the promotion of vocations as one of these non-negotiable goals. Almost every homily or address or pastoral letter should encourage the promotion of vocations to the priesthood.

The people should hear frequently that the entire community and every category within the community need the priest in order to be equipped for Christian living. Families, husbands and wives, parents, children, single persons, permanent deacons, religious men and women—all need the priestly ministry, because all Christian living, as the Second Vatican Council so powerfully proclaimed, has the Eucharist as "the source and summit of Christian living."

Pastoral visits to a parish provide a wonderful occasion to speak about vocations to the priesthood and at the same time to do so in a context that exalts the importance of *the Christian family.* It may be effective for the Bishop to point out publicly how many vocations have come from a given parish. He may want to name them and he may also want to remind the parish that there are no seminarians at the present time in the parish. He may wish to add words of praise for all the efforts that are made by the priests and their collaborators in promoting vocations. It is also good for the Bishop to report to the people that he, as the Bishop, would like to send another priest to the parish to help the community in their pastoral needs and that he would do this if he were in a position. Therefore, he needs more vocations from the parish itself. *A priest's funeral or jubilee* is another very appropriate time to promote the issue of vocation of priests.

It is important to give *the parents of priests* prominence during pastoral visits. This highlights the importance of families in fostering vocations.

Teachers in Catholic schools need to hear that the promotion of vocations to the priesthood is an expected part of their mandate. If a teacher in conscience says that he or she cannot promote vocations to the priesthood, then in conscience he or she should not teach in a Catholic school. There are certain Catholic schools that should be recognized and praised for the number of vocations that have come from their midst.

In creating the proper atmosphere, the Bishop must be *unapologetic* in promoting priestly vocations because the priestly vocation is at the service of every other vocation, and every other vocation needs the priesthood. The promotion of the laity and an emphasis on the universal call to holiness as well as the promotion of consecrated life should in no way silence the Bishop from appealing to the generosity of young men to follow Christ in the priesthood.

The Bishop must be especially vigorous in responding to the unfair charge that an aggressive promotion of priestly vocations demeans *the role of women* in the Church and demotes the laity. What is at stake is a correct understanding of the Body of Christ and its multiple charisms, all of which need and depend upon the priesthood.

Another role for the Bishop is to reject the opinion, which may sound plausible but which is in effect injurious to the life of the Church, that the shortage of vocations to the priesthood is really providential since it makes it necessary for the Church to come to more creative ways of offering pastoral leadership. This is usually a cover-up for advocating married and women priests. A healthy ecclesiology and conformity with the Second Vatican Council is an automatic refutation of this position. As mentioned, the Second Vatican Council opens the door and appeals to all to have an active and generous participation in the Church's life and in her mission of evangelization. There is *no dichotomy* in the Bishop's energetic promotion of vocations and his strong support of *the lay apostolate.*

The Role of the Family and the Priority of Prayer

In establishing a "pro-vocation" climate in his diocese, the Bishop must accent *the role of the family in fostering vocations.* In my estimation a very beautiful prayer of intercession is a prayer that God will give us more holy families, and that from holy families there may radiate an example to young people to be imbued with a true understanding of Christian married love and an esteem for the religious life and the priesthood of our Lord Jesus Christ.

In fostering a pro-vocation atmosphere in the diocese, the Bishop must have recourse to *the primacy of the supernatural.* In order words, the Bishop must stress *the priority of prayer,* which is, as we know, certainly not the entire strategy of the Church, but it is her great priority. The need for prayer is based upon her supernatural character and the command of the Lord: "Ask the master of the harvest to send our laborers for his harvest" (Luke 10:2).

There are different forms of *intercessory prayer for vocations*. In this regard there is no limit to the creativity of a Bishop and the local Church. Each local parish can respond with immense creativity. The Day of Prayer for Vocations set up by the Holy Father is a great opportunity to mobilize the diocese to draw attention, not only to *the need for vocations*, but to *the importance of the activity of the faithful in praying for vocations*. This is part of Christian life. This is an exigency of Christian discipleship for people of every vocation. They must share the solicitude of the Church to have priestly collaborators at the service of the community. An excellent practice exists of having *prayer vigils*. On different occasions people should be invited to pray specifically for vocations to the priesthood.

Eucharistic Adoration

Of immense importance in my estimation is the practice of *Eucharistic Adoration*. In the Synod for the Church in America I had the happy opportunity to speak on Eucharistic Adoration. I mentioned my conviction that the renewal of Eucharistic Adoration at this moment in the life of the Church is "a new emerging sign of the times." Bishops throughout the Church in different countries are speaking about this. Something is happening in the spirit of Vatican II, in the tradition of the Church and in total consonance with the Constitution on the Liturgy *Sacrosanctum Concilium*.

There is a new opportunity to stress that there should never be a dichotomy after Vatican II between the offering of the Eucharistic Sacrifice and the reservation and adoration of the Blessed Sacrament. The time has now come and is upon us to liquidate this dichotomy, wherever it may exist, showing that the Eucharistic celebration empowers the Church to go out and live Eucharistic generosity and return once again to celebrate the Eucharistic action. In the meantime, the Body and Blood of Christ made present truly and substantially in the Eucharist remain as the great expression of Christ's love and offer us the gift of his presence to be adored.

The testimony of the people is that the Eucharistic presence of Christ signifies for them strength in their Christian lives and gives them the wonderful opportunity for prayer, including intercessory prayer. *One of the major intentions of the intercessory prayer* of our people before the Blessed Sacrament should always be that of *vocations to the priesthood.*

Creative Pastoral Projects

When Pope John Paul II began his pontificate, he offered to the Church many marvelous examples of creative pastoral projects. Four of these I remember in particular. One of them was *to enthrone an image of Our Blessed Mother* in St. Peter's Square. The Holy Father installed a beautiful image of Mary under her title *Mater Ecclesiae.* It was installed on the building that houses the Secretariat of State and it is visible to everyone in St. Peter's Square.

The second initiative the Holy Father wanted was to establish a center of contemplative prayer in Vatican City. That he did by calling a series of contemplative communities to spend a period of five years in prayer at the seat of the universal Church to assist him, as Bishop of Rome, in his universal ministry of charity. So today we have the contemplative nuns within Vatican City.

Another creative project of the Pope was to establish *exposition of the Blessed Sacrament in St. Peter's Basilica*. He did this a number of years ago. Today, in the Chapel of the Blessed Sacrament, there is exposition of the Blessed Sacrament for a number of hours each weekday. Pope John Paul II and his predecessors—notably Paul VI—have always emphasized the social dimension of the Eucharist. Calling people to Eucharistic piety, to Eucharistic adoration, involves, in the mind of the Holy Father, a call to live the Eucharist through the application of the social teaching of the Church. We remember that the Eucharist was instituted on Holy Thursday at the same Supper during which Jesus gave his apostles the commandment of charity.

A fourth project of the Holy Father in Vatican City was to establish *a home for the poor*. And so the Holy Father called Mother Teresa to open the *Donum Mariae*, which would express the solicitude of the Church for the poor. Admittedly in the Diocese of Rome there are many institutions that care for the poor, many institutions that demonstrate the charity of Christ, and yet the Holy Father wanted something within the confines of Vatican City where the symbolism would not be lost and where Eucharistic piety would reveal one of its first fruits. All of this, dear brothers, shows a tremendous vision of the Holy Father, but all of it is Eucharistic. And just as the Eucharist is the source and summit of Christian life as it applies to the social teaching of the Church, so also *the Eucharist is the source and summit of the Christian life* as it applies to *the promotion of vocations to the priesthood*. The power of Christ's Paschal Mystery passes through the Eucharist and generates vocations to the priesthood. All of this involves

an act of faith on the part of the Church, beginning with
the Bishop.

In the silence of prayer and especially of Eucharistic
adoration, how much wisdom is imbibed by the People of
God! How much understanding of the nature of the
Church, of the nature of Christian living, of the nature of
their own vocation, do people acquire before Jesus in the
Blessed Sacrament! And how much, also, do they begin to
understand the plan of Christ for a Eucharistic Church and
for a Church dependent on the priestly ministry! Prayer
before the Eucharist is also the locus of the call for many
young men. In the history of the Church, how many young
men praying before the Eucharist have been given the
strength to make a further step of inquiry and response to
the call of Christ! In my estimation *the intercessory prayer of
Eucharistic adoration* cannot be overestimated in effectively
promoting vocations to the priesthood.

Inviting Priests to Promote Vocations

Another essential aspect of the Bishop's role in
promoting vocations that applies so much also to auxiliary
Bishops, is constantly *to invite the priests of the diocese
to be ambassadors of the call of Christ.* Imbued with this vision
of the Church, trusting in the power of the Paschal Mystery,
it is natural for the Bishop to share this most holy responsibility with his closest collaborators, the priests of the
diocese. On two different planes the Bishop and his priests
will continue to invite young men to the priesthood, but the
Bishop will be supremely conscious of the need to speak
frequently with his priests about such an important aspect
of their priesthood and of the Church. The Bishop's
ministry of promoting vocations to the priesthood, by its

nature, solicits and draws collaboration—the collaboration of priests, deacons, religious, and the laity. The spirit of joy with which all of these people pursue this holy cause is extremely important, but *the figure of the leader is of unique importance.*

The Example of Christian Joy

The Bishop himself must provide the example of a priest who is totally committed to the gift and mystery of the priesthood—one who is selfless in performing his tasks and one who rejoices even in tribulation. Christian joy is one of the greatest means to attract young men to the priesthood. *The person of the Bishop,* notwithstanding his human weaknesses and all his failings, is sacred. The person of the Bishop is *a sacred sign of the humanity of Christ* and it must reflect the joy that is in the heart of Christ. The only way it can reflect the joy of Christ is if the Bishop is living by faith and if the Bishop is convinced of the power of the Paschal Mystery of Christ to give the Church sufficient vocations for the needs of the local Church and the universal Church.

I believe, therefore, that the last word in the promotion of vocations to the priesthood on the part of the Bishop *is a renewed act of faith in the power of the Paschal Mystery.* It is from this act of faith in the efficacy of the Crucified and Risen Lord Jesus that there is unleashed a new wave of joyful trust. Under the action of the Holy Spirit this wave of joyful trust spreads from the Bishop to members of the local Church, including young men considering a vocation to the priesthood. Experience confirms that God so often works in this way.

39

The Bishop and the Pastoral Care of Seminarians

(Address to Newly Ordained Bishops, Part II
Rome, July 6, 2001)

Dear brother Bishops, dear Friends,

The pastoral care of seminaries involves *first and foremost* the pastoral care of *the seminarians*. Added to the seminarians are all those who make up the seminary community. In speaking about the Bishop's relationship to this community, and especially to the seminarians, the words of our Lord Jesus Christ himself come to mind: "I am the good shepherd, and I know mine and mine know me, just as the Father knows me and I know the Father; and I will lay down my life for the sheep" (John 10:14–15).

These words give us a tremendous insight into how the Bishop approaches his responsibility of the pastoral care that is his. It is imperative that the Bishop know his seminarians by name, even though this takes time to accomplish. Above all he must take an active interest in them and communicate this interest to them by his personal contact. Hence, the presence of the Bishop in the seminary is of great importance. Obviously, this is facilitated if the diocese has its own seminary. Even if it does not, the Bishop must make an effort to have contact with his seminarians to

the best of his ability, wherever they are. An annual
interview with at least a portion of the seminarians is
to be recommended.

Pastoral Visit to the Seminary

I was pleased to be able to inaugurate *a pastoral visit*
to my seminary, which also includes seminarians from some
twenty dioceses. It was a rewarding experience, giving
me the opportunity to have this personal contact, to listen
to the seminarians, to share their ideals. I sincerely hope
it confirmed them both in their faith and in their generous
resolution to be faithful to their vocation. A pastoral visit to
the seminary also involves personal contact with all those
who make up the seminary community.

The teachers are extremely important and the Bishop
needs to know to the extent possible what the seminarians
are being taught. In my own seminary it was an exhilarating
experience to hear seminarians tell me of their own personal conviction that the members of the seminary faculty
so faithfully teach according to the magisterium of the
Church. The combination of *true scholarship* and *fidelity to
the magisterium* is a component of priestly formation that
is so important.

Various Personal Contacts with the Bishop

So often it happens that a Bishop must send his
seminarians to a seminary outside his own diocese. It is easy
to forget to correspond with these seminarians and to exempt
them from corresponding with the Bishop. Yet, *this corre-
spondence* is part of the bond that is so necessary between
a Bishop and the seminarians, and which will help prepare
the seminarian to be part of a united presbyterate later on.

I find that with the advantage of having a seminary in my own archdiocese it is so useful to hold some other events with the seminarians outside of the seminary itself. One possibility is for the Bishop *to invite seminarians to his home.* This act fosters a close relationship between the Bishop and his seminarians. Some Bishops conduct days of recollection for their seminarians. Every contact immediately provokes in the seminarians gratitude and a real spirit of satisfaction in that it is an expression of a genuine relationship between the Bishop and the seminarian. The need for this is something that seminarians intuit, expect, and rejoice in.

It is an excellent practice *to have seminarians participate in the episcopal liturgies,* which give the people the opportunity to see the Bishop surrounded by seminarians. It is important to explain to the people on such occasions how important seminarians are in the life of the Church and in the plan of Christ for the salvation of the world.

At times it may be possible for the Bishop to supply his seminarians with *special publications.* Certainly this involves an expense and may not always be possible, but it may well be possible for the Bishop to organize the transmission, for example, of the Holy Father's Letter to Priests every Holy Thursday, ensuring that seminarians receive a copy of this document and are expected to read it. With the help of benefactors, it is sometimes possible to do more. In this way I was able at the time to supply all my seminarians and all the seminarians from other dioceses studying in my seminary with a copy of the revised *Catechism of the Catholic Church.* The letters of appreciation indicate that it was not only the utility of the work that was appreciated, but also the gesture of the Bishop.

Pastoral Encounters

How important it is before conferring the diaconate or the priesthood for the Bishop to have *an in-depth meeting with each candidate* to the extent possible. These are moments when the Bishop can truly show his pastoral charism, encouraging, and affirming the generosity that has brought the seminarian to this point. At the same time, these meetings are opportunities for the Bishop to be very explicit in reiterating the obligation of celibacy that seminarians assume and in giving his own testimony to the meaning of the commitment that the seminarian is undertaking to pastoral service and pastoral charity. These meetings give the Bishop the opportunity to speak of problems and challenges in the priesthood and confirm the candidates in confidence. The Bishop can emphasize all the responsibilities of the priesthood, but also all the grace that is given through the sacrament of Holy Orders. The Bishop is able not only to offer words of encouragement and instill an attitude of confidence, but so often it happens that the Bishop himself is confirmed in his own trust in God's providence, as he experiences how much generosity seminarians are capable of.

Once again this shows how necessary it is *that the Bishop himself exude confidence* in the power of the Paschal Mystery. He is able to speak with conviction, encouraging the seminarians to overcome all sorts of difficulties in this modern and pansexual society, because he relies on the power of Christ's grace to triumph in the hearts of young men. Once again, strong faith in the power of Christ's Paschal Mystery is essential.

In the Bishop's encounter with his seminarians there needs to be an extended dialogue about *the various dimensions of the spiritual life.* The Bishop must speak

about prayer and its challenges. It is important that
the seminarians receive from the Bishop an exhortation
to fidelity in praying the Liturgy of the Hours within
the realistic situation of pastoral ministry.

It is important for the Bishop to speak about the
Church's teaching on the sacrament of Holy Orders and
about the permanence of the priesthood. Seminarians need
to hear from the Bishop his acceptance of the Church's
teaching that the priesthood, in Christ's plan, is reserved to
men. The Archbishop of Chicago, Cardinal Francis George,
has insisted that his seminarians be able to explain this as
a condition for ordination to the priesthood. I believe that
it is essential for the Bishop to communicate *his own attitude of respect for the entire magisterium of the Church*, of
which he is a witness in communion with the Roman Pontiff.

Encouraging Seminarians to Witness to Vocations

Every contact of the Bishop with the seminarians
is an opportunity to instill in them *their role as promoters
of vocations*. They are very much ambassadors of Christ and
the example of their own fidelity is a wonderful attraction to
other young people. We remember the attraction of sanctity
that so touched Saint Augustine in his conversion as he
said to himself: *"Tu non poteris quod isti et istae."* Seminarians,
hence, are to be encouraged by the Bishop to do everything
possible to let their light shine before others so that other
young men may see their good works and generosity
and realize that what is possible for the seminarian is
possible for the prospective seminarian. And, whereas *the
power of example* is the greatest of all elements in attracting
vocations, the power of the word is not to be underesti-
mated. Young people themselves are to be encouraged to

speak about their vocations and to share with others the fulfillment that comes from following Christ. Obviously this takes modesty and humility, but it also takes enthusiasm and the conviction that "It is impossible for us not to speak about what we have seen and heard" (Acts 4:20).

The Bishop's Doctrinal Understanding of the Priesthood

A Bishop's vigilance over the seminary is governed by his own clear doctrinal understanding of the priesthood. The education that he fosters in the seminary aims at ensuring a secure priestly identity according to the mind and the heart of the Church. In this regard the Bishop himself goes back repeatedly to the magisterium of the Church. The Bishop recalls the explicit teaching of the Second Vatican Council in its decree on priestly formation, *Optatam Totius.* *Optatam Totius* guides the Bishop as he in turn guides and inspires the seminary faculty with great confidence according to the mind of the Second Vatican Council. The pastoral care of the Bishop emphasizes the need for *the spiritual formation* that is closely linked with *the human, intellectual, disciplinary, doctrinal, and pastoral training* of candidates for the priesthood—all according to the Second Vatican Council. The same decree of priestly formation speaks about the importance of seminarians being imbued with the mystery of the Church and with the mystery of Christ.

These topics furnish the Bishop with splendid opportunities to teach and to evangelize the seminarians, assisting them to reach the fullness of the formation that the Church wishes them to have. The wisdom of the Second Vatican Council which directs priestly formation is further embellished and applied in the post-synodal apostolic exhortation *Pastores Dabo Vobis.* This document has exquisite insights into the question of priestly formation and the role of the Bishop in this regard. This document insists that the training for the priesthood is essentially *the preparation of future shepherds in the likeness of Jesus Christ,* the Good Shepherd, and that Jesus Himself, through the outpouring of His Spirit, gives and develops in candidates for the priesthood the pastoral charity that he himself lived to the point of total self-giving (cf. John 15:13).

Representing Christ to the Seminarians and the Seminary

In addition, *Pastores Dabo Vobis* also develops beautifully the theme of the Bishop as being *a representative of Christ Himself* in the priestly formation of His priests. *Pastores Dabo Vobis* applies to the Bishop—obviously in a subordinate manner—the passage of Saint Mark that recounts the call of Jesus to His apostles: He "summoned those whom he wanted; and they came to him. He appointed twelve . . . that they might be with him, and he might send them forth . . ." (Mark 3:13–14). The post-synodal apostolic exhortation, in applying these words—*to be with him*—to the Bishop, emphasizes so greatly the need for the presence of the Bishop in the seminary.

The Bishop is encouraged to give significant expression to his responsibility for the formation of candidates for the priesthood. In particular, the document says: "The presence of the Bishop is especially valuable, not only because it helps the seminary community live its insertion in the particular church and its communion with the pastor who guides, but also because it verifies and encourages the pastoral purpose which is what specifies the entire formation of candidates for the priesthood" (*Pastores Dabo Vobis*, 65). This document is so important not only for the norms it gives, but also for the underlying spirit of the relationship which it prescribes for the Bishop to have with the seminary and in particular with the seminarians. The Bishop represents Christ the Pastor, Christ the Shepherd, who through His Spirit forms seminarians in His own pastoral office and engenders in them His own pastoral charity. This principle explains and clarifies so much of our theme: *The Bishop and the Pastoral Care of Seminaries.*

The Bishop's role of vigilance and personal participation is totally guided by the principle that *he represents Christ.* In those dioceses that have their own seminary, how important it is that the Bishop appoint a rector who personifies his own vision of the priesthood, understood in the sense of the Church's vision of the priesthood, the total vision of the Church expressed in *Optatam Totius* and *Pastores Dabo Vobis* and in so many other documents of Pope Paul VI and Pope John Paul II that implement the genuine teaching of the Second Vatican Council.

A Partnership in Preparing Seminarians

It is not possible to pursue the pastoral aim of the seminary in all its effectiveness unless the Bishop is vigilant in regard to the appointment of *the faculty* who firmly and enthusiastically are committed to the Church's teaching, especially on the priesthood. In a pastoral visit it is a joy to speak to the seminary faculty about their role and to encourage them in the *partnership* that they have with the Bishop in helping to prepare candidates for the priesthood.

Frequent visits to the seminary—announced and unannounced—on the part of the Bishop can be extremely useful. My own visits are generally announced. Most often they include the celebration of the Eucharist with the seminarians and the entire community. On some occasions there is the celebration of the Eucharist with other groups that join the seminarians. Sometimes there are groups of priests who celebrate anniversaries at the seminary. A visit to the seminary by members of *the diocesan presbyterate* is a blessing to the seminarians. The attention of the seminarians should be drawn by the Bishop personally to the example of priests who have generously, joyfully, and perseveringly fulfilled their ministry.

It is understood that the Bishop trusts the rector of his seminary, the faculty whom he chooses, and the other collaborators who generously assist him in the seminary. This does not, however, exempt him from a personal contribution to *the seminary board,* where it exists, and from taking an active interest in both *the planning of the curriculum and its execution.* He is also responsible for the major policies of the seminary and should certainly be concerned with the important role of assuming the more important faculty members.

In dioceses that have their own seminary, the Bishop is faced with the task of sacrificing some of his most talented priests for appointment to the seminary. This was the advice years ago of Pope Pius XI in his encyclical *Ad Catholici Sacerdotii.* His words to the Bishops ring out in subsequent ecclesial documents, "Put your best priests in the seminary." Obviously Bishops are bound by so many demands. We are called to act within the context of what is possible, and sometimes this is not the ideal. But one thing we know is that the work of a priest and the service that he gives to the Church as the rector of the seminary or a member of the seminary faculty is *a pastoral contribution of supreme importance.* The formation of other shepherds for the Church is something essential to the mission of Christ and his entire Body.

Pre-eminence of the Seminary Apostolate and the Collegial Spirit

It is so important for Bishops in their pastoral care of seminaries to have the deep personal conviction that all the investment of time, personal energy, finances, and personnel in the seminary is a direct contribution to the Church's mission of evangelization, education, and charity. The priest is necessary for every community because the Eucharist is necessary, and without the priest there is no Eucharist. Hence, every effort must be made to form shepherds after the heart of Christ. In the words of Vatican II, every program of instruction in the seminary is directed to this end and contributes to the community of the Church (cf. *OT,* 4).

Many Bishops are in a different situation where they do not possess a diocesan seminary and yet their role can be one of great contribution to the seminary that accepts their students. What I mentioned in regard to personal contacts applies even outside the diocese. It obviously involves even more effort for the Bishop. It is important that the Bishop delegate a diocesan vocations director to visit the seminarians, and yet we know that his own presence to the extent possible is also required. Some seminaries that are interdiocesan or that, while they are a diocesan seminary, offer services to other dioceses as my own does, require the presence on the board of trustees of other Bishops.

What a splendid service this is when Bishops from different dioceses assume, *in a collegial spirit,* the responsibility of assisting a central seminary in its work of formation by their presence on the board. Such an institution gives encouragement to the Bishop of the diocese in which the seminary is located. Participating Bishops give pastoral insights to the process of reviewing and consolidating the type of formation that is given in the seminary. Every manifestation of the collegial spirit is a great gift to God's people.

A Community of Truth and Holiness

I remember years ago—back in 1977—how Pope Paul VI encouraged the Bishops of the United States of America in their pastoral responsibility to seminaries. On that occasion he said, "Venerable brothers, we beseech you to guard the content of the Catholic and apostolic faith. Speak about it often to your people. Discuss it with your priests and deacons and religious. We ask you to fulfill with loving personal attention your great pastoral responsibility to your seminarians: know the content of their courses, encourage them to love the Word of God and never be ashamed of the seeming folly of the cross" (June 20, 1977).

To know the content of their courses! Obviously this is a great challenge that the Bishop begins to fulfill by his deep interest in the seminary and by his conversations with seminarians and faculty members, who know his own values, are encouraged by his apostolic fidelity, and share with him on different occasions their own insights into the faith. As dialogue and exchange develops between the community of the seminary and the Bishop, and as the seminary community is instructed, nourished, and affirmed by the

Bishop, who speaks with apostolic clarity and in total consonance with the teaching and tradition of the Church, especially as it is expressed in the Second Vatican Council, there is an increase in mutual trust and an ever greater sense of communion in the local Church.

The pastoral care of the Bishop for seminaries truly involves a contribution to *building up a true community* that lives in virtue of the communion of the Church, which is the communion of the Most Blessed Trinity, and this is needed in the life of candidates for the priesthood. *Seminarians must experience in the seminary the communion of the Church* in order to be effective pastors of the Church. But first they must experience the role of the disciples as described in the third chapter of Saint Mark's Gospel. The candidates for the priesthood must experience *being with Christ.* As *Pastores Dabo Vobis* points out, they have this experience through the Bishop, and it is through this experience of being with Christ that they will then be in a position as priests to proclaim the Gospel and build up the Church.

Brothers, the pastoral care of seminaries and the promotion of vocations are really *exhilarating dimensions of our pastoral ministry,* whether we be ordinaries or auxiliary Bishops. All of this obviously requires the assistance of the Holy Spirit. How wonderful to think that within this last year all of you have received this gift of the Holy Spirit. You have received the Holy Spirit in order to fulfill the pastoral mission of the Church, which is *to communicate Christ* to the world. This task, brothers, you fulfill eminently in your dedicated pastoral care of seminaries and in your promotion of vocations to the priesthood of Jesus Christ.

40

Identity and Spirituality of Priests and Bishops

(Address to the United States Bishops,
St. Louis, June 20, 2003)

Dear Brothers, dear Friends,

The topic of *the identity and spirituality of priests and Bishops* involves our whole lives, everything we stand for, everything we have tried to be. So our own experience means a great deal to us. Yet, after reflecting on various dimensions of our lives, we can take a fresh look at familiar Scripture passages and the teaching of the Church to be ever more confirmed in our convictions and to understand more deeply *who we are* and *how we are to live*.

Right away I would suggest that in reflecting on the *identity and spirituality* of priests and Bishops, we are not talking about everything that a priest or Bishop is expected to do in the Church today. I do not believe that we are able to spell out every aspect of our multifaceted ministry, every obligation that we have, every need of our people that affects us, or every burden of our people that we strive to share.

We are speaking about *who* priests and bishops are and who they are meant to be as ministers of God's word, set apart like Saint Paul "to proclaim the Gospel of

God" (Romans 1:1). It seems to me that *the realization of our identity* is then the key to the understanding of *how* we are to live in the Church: in other words, *our spirituality*.

Profound Simplicity

We should not be surprised if the simple evangelical and ecclesial insights that we may wish to confirm after our reflection on our identity and spirituality may be challenged as being too simplistic. Indeed our whole view of the human person, our Christian anthropology, is not readily accepted by a world that exalts action over being, a world that embraces pragmatism, functionalism, and utilitarianism. What the Church may consider simple, the world may certainly judge simplistic.

I am reminded of the story of Naaman as recorded in the Second Book of Kings. He was the army commander of the King of Aram in Syria, and he had leprosy. Word came that there was a prophet in Israel who could make him clean. The King of Aram sent letters with Naaman to the King of Israel, who in turn spoke to the prophet Elisha. Elisha's message to Naaman was simple and direct: "Go and wash seven times in the Jordan and your flesh will heal, and you will be clean." We are told that Naaman reacted angrily: "I thought that he would surely come out and stand there to invoke the Lord his God, and would move his hand over the spot, and thus cure the leprosy. Are not the rivers of Damascus, the Abana and the Pharpar, better than all the waters of Israel? Could I not wash in them and be cleansed?" We are told: "With this he turned about in anger and left." It was his servants who reasoned with him: "My father, if the prophet had told you to do something extraordinary, would you not have done it? All the more now, since

he said to you, 'Wash and be clean,' should you do as he
said." We know the rest, how Naaman obeyed, was made
clean and confessed: "Now I know . . . " (2 Kings 5:1–5).

The parallel between the case of Naaman and our
own challenge is perhaps the need to recognize *the simplicity
of the divine plan*. Concentrating on our identity will lead
us to reaffirm and understand more fully our spirituality. It
will not, however, remove the immense challenges we face.
It will not make easy all the numerous tasks that weigh
upon us, except in the profoundly supernatural sense intended
by Jesus, when He says, "My yoke is easy and my burden
light" (Matthew 11:30). And so what is this identity? What
is this spirituality?

At the Heart of What It Means To Be a Priest

There are many documents of the magisterium that
can enlighten us, in particular Vatican II's *Presbyterorum
Ordinis,* the Post Synodal Apostolic Exhortation *Pastores Dabo
Vobis,* and various *Ad Limina* addresses of the Holy Father
to the Bishops of the United States.

To both priests and Bishops, the Church consistently
offers the Good Shepherd as the exemplar of their identity.
John Paul II, concluding his own reflections in *Pastores
Dabo Vobis* says, "Dear brother priests, . . . our Lord himself,
with the strength of his Spirit, has called you to incarnate in the earthen vessels of your simple lives the priceless
treasure of his Good Shepherd's love" (no. 82). Earlier,
the Holy Father spoke about "the ontological bond which
unites the priesthood to Christ the High Priest and Good
Shepherd" (no. 11).

In an *Ad Limina* address to the Bishops of the
United States (September 9, 1983), the Holy Father outlined

various elements that make up the priest's *Good Shepherd ministry.* His words reveal his own personal experience:

"Even after years of experiencing the joys attached to a vast number of apostolic activities, we can look back and say that our greatest strength and the deepest source of gladness for our hearts has been *the daily celebration of Mass,* beginning with those early days after our priestly ordination. And we have always been convinced that the Eucharist is our most outstanding contribution to the Church, our greatest priestly service to the people, the deepest meaning of that splendid vocation which we share with our brother priests."

The Pope went on to add: "Only the priesthood can furnish the Eucharist to God's people. And only priests have the wonderful opportunity to serve God's people by supplying them with the bread of life. . . ."

At this point John Paul II quoted from a pastoral letter of one of the American Bishops saying that this Bishop "expressed so much of the Church's understanding of the priesthood in the following terms: 'The priestly ministry requires us to do many things: to preach the Word of God, to minister the other Sacraments, to encourage, to console, to serve human need, to serve the Church in administration, which the New Testament numbers among the charisms, and to do a variety of other things in virtue of the mission we receive from the Church. This means, of course, that the priesthood does not consist exclusively in the celebration of the Eucharist. And yet, if we reflect carefully on the Church's faith about the essential link between the Sacrament of Holy Orders and the Eucharist, it does mean that the celebration of the Eucharist is at the heart of what it means to be a priest. It means that somehow and in an ultimate way the priest finds his identity in this link

between his Priesthood and the Eucharist.'" The Holy
Father then identified his source as Archbishop John Quinn.

Continuing on, he told the Bishops that "in
moments of calm and in times of crisis, we must assert the
priorities of the priesthood." He further affirmed: ". . . if
we read carefully the signs of the times as they relate to the
priesthood, we will discern that the Eucharist determines
the meaning of the priesthood and the identity of our priests.
The Council is clear and concise. Its testimony means so
much to clarify the meaning of our priesthood, to shed
light on postconciliar questionings and theological reflections.
Let us all listen again, together with our presbyterates. It is
the Holy Spirit speaking through the Council and saying:
'Priests fulfill their chief duty in the mystery of the
Eucharistic Sacrifice. In it the work of our redemption
continues to be carried out' (*Presbyterorum Ordinis*, 13). It is
crystal clear today and for the future: the priesthood is forever linked to the Eucharistic Sacrifice and to the actuation
of the Redemption."

No Greater Fulfillment

"But the Eucharist is also linked to the building of
community. Here too all our priests can fulfill their divine
vocation and their human aspirations. Through our priests,
each local community is built up in faith and charity,
and in an openness to the universal Church. . . .

"In the Eucharistic Sacrifice the priest finds the
source of all his pastoral charity (cf. *Presbyterorum Ordinis*,
14). The spirituality of all diocesan and religious priests
is linked to the Eucharist. Here they obtain the strength to
make the offering of their lives together with Jesus, High

Priest and Victim of salvation. Through the Eucharistic Sacrifice, celibacy is confirmed and strengthened."

John Paul II then spoke about other *identifying elements* of the priesthood: "In every age of the Church there are many meaningful actuations of the priestly ministry. But after the Eucharist, what could be more important than the *'ministry of reconciliation'* (2 Corinthians 5:18) as exercised in the sacrament of Penance? What greater human fulfillment is there than touching human hearts through the power of the Holy Spirit and in the name of the merciful and compassionate Redeemer of the world? Like the laity, our priests must strive to serve in many relevant ways every day, but they alone can forgive sins in the name of the Lord Jesus. And connected with the forgiveness of sins is new life and hope and joy for the People of God.

"With fidelity to Christ, in whose 'person' he acts, the priest realizes his identity and mission also through the Liturgy of the Hours, through different forms of prayer, through the reading of the word of God and through the oblation of his will, made in union with that of Christ. The priest's special love will always be with the sick and dying, with those in pain and sorrow, and with those in sin. For every Bishop and priest there is but one ideal—the person who says, 'I am the good shepherd . . . and I lay down my life for the sheep'" (John 10:14–15).

Once again we return to *the image of the Good Shepherd.* Implicit in this identification of the priestly ministry is the fact that the priest always works in union with the Church and his Bishop. On their part Bishops exercise their ministry in collegiality, in fraternal care and solicitude for the whole Church, which is missionary by nature. Bishops are chosen by Christ to be a group, to be a body, to be a College. Our relationships in the Episcopal Conference are part of the way in which we live out the mystery of our being chosen to evangelize together.

Our Whole Life Is Pastoral Charity

Pastores Dabo Vobis pointed out further that the priest's identity has its source in the Blessed Trinity and is realized in the Church. It states: "It is within the Church's mystery, as a mystery of Trinitarian communion in missionary tension, that every Christian identity is revealed, and likewise the specific identity of the priest and his ministry" (no. 12).

Reflection on our identity leads us to the spirituality that flows from it. This is above all *Trinitarian* and *Eucharistic*. It is also *Marian* because it goes back to Calvary and to Pentecost.

The spirituality of the priest is described at length in Chapter III of *Pastores Dabo Vobis,* which insists that priests have *a specific vocation to holiness* because they are configured to Christ the Head and Shepherd of the Church. Christ's whole life is one of *pastoral charity.* So is the life of the priest and bishop who represents Christ the Shepherd.

The *essential content of pastoral charity* is the total gift of self to the Church, after the example of Christ the Shepherd. Jesus Himself in the Gospel of Saint John tells us about His own pastoral charity. Five times in chapter ten He speaks about "laying down his life." And then He reveals the full meaning of pastoral charity when He says, "This is why the Father loves me because I lay down my life . . ." (John 10:17).

Part of *the Good Shepherd spirituality* is being obedient to the Church as Christ was obedient to the Father. This obedience recognizes, loves, and serves the Church in her hierarchical structure and is motivated to benefit the whole flock. Pastoral charity is ignited and evoked by the needs of God's people.

"The Church, as the Spouse of Jesus Christ, wishes," John Paul II states, "to be loved by the priest in the total and exclusive manner in which Jesus Christ, her Head and Spouse loved her. Priestly celibacy, then, is the gift of self in and with Christ to the Church . . ." (no. 29). In celibacy, human sexuality continues to be a service to the love of communion and a gift of self to others.

In Need of Conversion

One further factor of priestly spirituality greatly emphasized by *Pastores Dabo Vobis* is the need for *conversion* and *reconciliation* in the Sacrament of Penance. The Pope quotes another Synod, saying: "The priest's spiritual and pastoral life . . . depends, for its quality and fervor, on the frequent and conscientious personal practice of the Sacrament of Penance. The priest's celebration of the Eucharist and administration of other Sacraments, his pastoral zeal, his relationship with the faithful, his communion with his brother priests, his collaboration with his Bishop, his life of prayer—in a word, the whole of his priestly existence, suffers an inexorable decline if by negligence or for some other reason he fails to receive the Sacrament of Penance at regular intervals and in a spirit of genuine faith and devotion. If a priest were no longer to go to confession or properly confess his sins, his priestly being and his priestly action would feel its effects very soon, and this would also be noticed by the community of which he was the pastor" (no. 26).

Another beautiful and specific element of priestly spirituality the Holy Father presents is the awareness of "being in a particular Church."

So much of priestly spirituality is summarized *in friendship with Jesus.* After all, the original call of the Apostles was to be with him and to be sent out (cf. Mark 3:14).

Finally in order to avoid any vestige of Pelagianism in speaking about priestly spirituality, the Holy Father clearly recognizes the Holy Spirit as *the principal agent of our spiritual life.* Sent by Jesus and the Father, He is the Spirit of holiness in our lives as we are configured to the Good Shepherd.

A separate issue that would merit attention is the need for vocations. The Holy Father's position is this ". . . in the face of a crisis of priestly vocations the first answer which the Church gives lies in a total act of faith in the Holy Spirit" (no. 1). The Holy Father characterizes this as the "first answer" and obviously not the "whole answer." He also adds the need for "total trust in God's unconditional faithfulness to his promise," the need for prayer, and the work necessary to face the situation (cf. no. 2).

To Incarnate the Priceless Treasure of the Good Shepherd's Love

In addition to the above reflections which concern the identity and spirituality of both priests and Bishops, John Paul II has developed at some length, in another *Ad Limina* address (September 5, 1983), his reflections— beginning with a reflection on the Good Shepherd— on *the specific identity of the Bishop and the elements of his spiritual life.*

It is a daily source of strengthening joy and inspiration to keep in mind the vision of Pope John Paul II as he describes the Bishop (who is always, together with his priests,):

- "a living sign of Jesus Christ"
  (This requires personal conversion and holiness of life);

- "a sign of the love of Jesus Christ"
  (This involves the love of understanding and consolation);

- "a sign of Christ's love for his priests"
  (The Bishop manifests to priests the love of friendship);

- "a sign of Christ's compassion";

- "a sign of Christ's truth"
  (He must proclaim without fear or ambiguity the many controverted truths of our age. He must discern in union with the universal Episcopate the signs of the times);

- "a sign of fidelity to the doctrine of the Church";

- "a sign of the certainty of faith."

The Pope goes on to say, "Called to proclaim salvation in Jesus Christ and to lead the flock effectively to this goal, the Bishop inculcates certainty in the people of God, who know that he will listen to them, accept their numerous insights into the truth of the faith, and impose no unnecessary burdens on their lives. And yet they know that the Church's teaching which he announces is much more than human wisdom. The Church, through her Bishops, rejects all triumphalism; she publicly denies that she has ready-made solutions to all particular problems, but she definitely claims to possess the light of revealed truth— which transcends all human consensus—and she works with all her strength so that this light of faith will illumine the experiences of humanity (cf. *Gaudium et Spes*, 33)."

The Pope then points out that the Bishop is called to be:

- "a teacher of prayer and a living sign of the praying Christ"
- "a sign of the unity of the universal Church"
- "a sign of Catholic solidarity"
- "a sign of contradiction"
- "a sign of hope for the people of God, as strong and unbreakable as the sign of the cross, becoming a living sign of the Risen Christ."

At the end, the Holy Father returns yet again to the image of the *Good Shepherd,* speaking in encouraging words about the many holy Bishops who, with their priests, live and die "so that Jesus Christ, the Good Shepherd may continue to lead his people to the newness of life and the fullness of salvation."

May the presence of Jesus Christ, the Good Shepherd, be readily seen in the midst of His people through the unity of our priests and Bishops, and through our friendship. And may we find an ever deeper joy in our priesthood!